The Creation OF OZZY FROM tHE ALtERS OF HiS BLACK SABBAtH

The Myths and Naked Truths

Steven Machat

The School of
Sacred Knowledge

ISBN-13 : 978-1-64136-152-1
ISBN-10: 1-64136-152-2

This book is published by The School of Sacred Knowledge.
For more information about The School of Sacred Knowledge please write us
The School of Sacred Knowledge c/o Steven Machat
100 Farm Road
Summertown, TN 38483

The school of sacred
knowledge series.

The creation of myths.
The perpetuation of
those lies.

Cast of Characters

Usual Ozzie cast

Supporting cast

John Michael Osborne

Sharon Levy aka Sharon Arden aka Sharon is Bourne

Thelma Riley

Pope Innocentius VIII
Heinrich Kramer
Jakob Sprenger
Jesus
Christ
Pope Honorius III
Harold Levy aka Don Arden
David Levy aka David Arden
Osiris
Isis
Typhoon
Orpheus
Randy Rhodes
Bob Daisley
Lee kerslake
Hitler
King George VI
Hope Shaw aka Pat Arden
Martin Machat
Kray Twins
Robin Hood
King Arthur

Brutus
Peter Grant
Led Zeppelin
Robert Stigwood
The Animals
Micke Most
Patrick Meehan Sr and JR
Jim Simpson
Black Sabbath
Bill Ward
Geezer Butler
Tony Iommi
The Move
Roy Wood
Jeff Lynne
ELO
Barrón Machat

And very humbly I add myself Steven Machat as the fixer.

Epilogue:

The Druids Priest and Bards
Herodotus
Strabo
Cicero
Caesar

Special Thanks

To Brian Forbes my Literary Guide and his daughters Jordan and Shayna for being there.

To Debbie Veltri my special editor and my Debbie.

To Jeannie Leto my metaphysical tour guide.

And to my Russian crew Alex and Olga.

To Ken Levine. A cheerleader of all games.

To Michael Garbutt. For being

To the farm Albert Jason and Millie

To my spirits whom encouraged my writing this book. Dad aka Martin Machat. Don Harold Arden. And Arthur Pollack,

To Mom aka Roslyn Machat.

To Barrón. My son who lost his physical life trying to make a myth with me.

To Margaux my daughter who is searching still

And to our Creator. I am so happy you made me hear that day when I rediscovered you the song " In the presence of the Lord.

I share each breath I get here trying to encourage people to believe in themselves.

Table of Contents

Part One

Ozzy Osbourne.
A Rock N Roll Truth?
A Rock N Roll Deception? Both?

Myths vs Truths.

The myth is Ozzie. At earth birth he was proclaimed to be John Michael Osbourne. Little did his earth creators know that John, now Ozzy, would be the prized prince of darkness.

Saying the word Ozzy excites an energy of angst inside his followers who question a society of rules and order. Yet, he and his Queen, Sharon, as well as their offspring live off you as you believe they are the instruments of change instead of being the magnets to take your change. You give them your trinkets and they just laugh and live their lives taking and taking what they can where they can.

John the man was born December 3, 1948 into an England just out of a world war where the country united to save their fairy tale land with Kings and Queens. Princes and Princesses. Dukes and Earls. A concept called an Empire where the sun was somewhere up and shining around our globe. Meaning the sun then did not set on their English/British Empire. That Truth would sure end. Piece by piece. And when the end came death followed. What happened in India being split up into East Pakistan, India and West Pakistan is a crime of which we are never taught. We should be taught as millions died and for what? But in that empirical tirade the minions in Britain did not care as they were still under the myth of Rudyard Kipling and his poetry of pure darkness, the white man's burden (aka WASP).

The English love myths. They love the concept of their kingdom. The kingdom meant to control mankind's trade amongst each other in a one world global order. An order where everything from time zones to financial institutions revolve around people believing this is what the god that controls our world wants.

But to prove your view in a world of controlling lives based on myths you need a god and you need a jester. That is, the more jesters the better if you can. So hello music in the 1960's. The British Invasion.

The underlying theme here is the creation of the jester of darkness and how it happened. To create the thought, you must give it air and then get that thought into its orbit so you can see its light or shadows.

I am not placing blame on anyone. Just telling my truths as in this creation game of Oz. I was the fixer. The fixer who swept all the insanity under carpets until I could not take it anymore.

In fact, I love people and what we believe and why we believe it amuses me. I have spent my life learning people and making dreams come true as well as burying dreams that time would not let happen. But if you believe in yourself never stop. You came to this planet as an ego to have your dream. My advice is get it if you can. But learn universal truths as you continue the sin of living your individual ego, where you edge god out. I did and I paid for it which is why I now have the School of Sacred Knowledge. A school dedicated to sharing those universal truths which are known by those who are known and hidden by them so they can rule in their private club over you.

Visualize it is 1971 and England is in trouble. The Empire is lost and now the pieces are cracking too. Unemployment is rampant. But the schools in the country teach you how myths come about. They teach you how to dream and then live your dream. Hence the flow of singers and songwriters that got off the UK shores in our 1960's.

Black Sabbath was one of those bands. In 1971 when the band, in which John sang, was breaking (meaning known around the world) John got married. John was married to a lady known before as Thelma Riley. That marriage lasted 11 years with two children. That marriage lasted in name from 1971 through 1982. 1982 is when Sharon got involved with the band known as Blizzard of Ozz. John, now known only as Ozzy, was the lead singer. The band was tight. It had great players and musicians who could write the songs needed to intoxicate you in their intellectual perfume, so you followed their moves. Worship is the better term.

The stage was set. The players were lined up and working without realizing a new English myth was about to be created. The creation of the new god, the gangsters who would create this myth, be they warlocks or witches, and you had the fixer who helped create a world that hid the truths in plain view.

Now I must share with you some metaphysical truths.

What is a god? An existence that individuals believe in and therefore follow. God can be a thought, possession or thing as well as a person.

What is a gangster? The enforcer of the god. The enforcer can be male and sometimes called a warlock or can be female and most females are also known as witches.
What is a witch?

A witch is one who use their feminine charm to make others become more than they were in the eyes of those about to be intoxicated by the spell of the myth. This feminine superpower is not good for a world based on a set controlling caste system order. .

A woman can change the world others knew and live on and off that earlier creation. I love women and I admire feline energy. No woman no baby cry.

Witch's became the bad women when the Vatican had their dark European ages falling apart. The printing press hit their European continent.

Just to get you really into this story that follows I must share the following.

It's 1484 or there about. The Pope Innocentius VIII, had a problem with women learning to read, and trying to get an equal setting in the communities of mankind. This did not sit well in the 'men's club' called the Catholic Church which was heavily engaged in the slave trading of Africans. In fact, this Pope was the son of the Viceroy of Naples which is where the majority of the Slave trade to Europe then took place. The Pope calls upon two German Inquisitors named

Heinrich Kramer and Jakob Sprenger to discover the power of women. Their dark side. The side that makes men follow love, which Jesus spoke of. But the Jesus spirit of love is the myth. The reality is the Church is about Christ control.

These two men with the blessings of Christ and with Jesus crying out loud no no no created the myth of witches. Witches are those women who howl at the moon. Those who can make men crazy and destroy communities blinded by the false myths of Jesus now known as Christ. These two, with Christ as their guide, demonstrate that witches are members of Satan's harem.ie natural state of witches. All witchcraft they write comes from carnal
lust, which in women is insatiable. The two warn that such beings of pleasant aspect, fetid retouch and deadly company enchant men and attract them, use their voices as a hiss, their Scorpion tale hidden in their ass that sways as men go ahhhh. Game is to lure them in and annihilate them into disrespecting Christ. As love is not the answer, control is the game. These witches change the control from the church to the lovers in their quest to make a new world which they can run and play and believe in this love and their dream in their present lifetime.

This treatise on witches then known as Malleus Maleficarum now called the Hammer of Witches then taught you the techniques to remove in an exorcism these tittied creatures' demons with their long hair.

The Vatican, as Christ guided this writing, recommended the following punishment. First everyone suspected of being a witch was to be tortured. Beaten. Those who then confessed deserved the stake which not like Jesus who was hung for really being a warlock, no these titty creatures were to be burned so their milk went back to earth.

Those who did not confess got the stake and were burnt too. Why? Because in the Vatican's visions of Christ they heard those who do not confess are being fortified by her lover Satan, who inspires these witches at their Black Sabbath could resist confessing with this torture. They are still the devil's angels.

In the 1200's a Pope named Honorius III said that women should not speak. The vocals that come out of their mouths carry the stigma of Eve, which lead mankind to its perdition.

So here we are eight centuries later and still the Catholic Church denies women the pulpit.

And just sharing truth with you today's world the fundamentalist Muslims still mutilate genitalia, plus cover the women's faces and cover their bodies. The same things nuns do today too.

Orthodox Jews are no better. Look what they do to their partner in creation. Look at their black clothing they wear and covered heads. The hit fashion of the 13th century East European ghettos. Each morning when the men arise they say prayers to god, thanking their god, a man, that they are not a woman.

I write this to tell you that to me this is all BS. A woman who uses power to educate or change situations is called a witch by the inferior minds of men who are losing the way they thought it should always be. If a man questioned authority it was easy, they would just kill him for not being one of us. A woman, the only asset mankind has, (i.e. the womb) was not one they could just kill so they needed Christ's permission. I love women and one day when we acknowledge that feminine energy must ride side by side with the masculine energy our world will change. Then we will have the empire our consciousness wished to create for all under the sun in this created heaven. Heaven of health and happiness called earth.

Back to the 70's. John the man became Ozzy the prince of darkness. His creator Don Arden with the help of his son David and daughter Sharon created the Blizzard of Oz, which I killed off for business reasons, to launch into the skies- Ozzy. But like all

things creation there needed to be a female partner. Some call it a witch but I call it the energy to make sure the creation survives. This is the story that I lived and which Sharon did not want to come out. Ozzy himself was the maker of his solo existence. Ozzy would not conform. Ozzy was a rebel. Sharon did rein him in.

So the way to make a god is taught in the schools of England. Here is one of those stories which perpetuates the imperial rule of kingdoms with their royal retinue.

No creation is an island. Even our one Creator had to break into a he and she. That, my friends, is the Hindu story of creation. All physical life's physical creator is the one with the womb. As the womb is where physical creation takes hold.

But as we begin I feel it important to first share with you the myth. This myth is central to the imperial education that is taught in the Uk to justify the way the isles built their world on the backs of others. The man-made god with the priests and royalty and laws built to protect the matrix said this is how god wants it. And because we believe it to be so, in reality becomes the illusions of lies that we believe and make the thoughts our living reality.

Understanding this genesis today called capitalism shows why we do the things we do. Hence the current story of how

John the man became Ozzy the legend and Sharon his handler.

So who in this myth was the creator of earthlings and the creator of all of mankind.

The birth of Osiris. The 21st century version.

From the midst of Chaos was born Osiris. At the moment of birth the words were heard, so says the legend, by whom we do not know, so maybe the announcement was to the energy of the Universe "The Ruler of the earth was born".

However Osiris was not the only creation. He was first. Second of that womb came Isis the Queen of her light. Then we need one more, so those two, a man and a womb man were followed by Typhon.

Now in the myth, Osiris alive in human form, travels the world. Out of nowhere the world is populated by many who just live. Those living then enjoy the blessings of nature as children do. That is until we put them into our schools of brainwashing thoughts and make them part of the class system. A universal earth class system we live in but deny exists. And this requires a myth that gets you to believe this is why you exist. Conform and behave.

We are taught to do as we are told. If you obey, no questioning and you may become one of us. Oh what a wonderful world this becomes. Again, I repeat you do as you're told if you believe the source of the command is better than you.

You see as we experience earth without mankind's control we learn these truths. No manmade god but nature itself gives us herbs and vegetables. Nature gives us trees that bear us fruit, Nature creates the streams which quench our thirst and give us fish to eat. We learn from the grasses growing wild on the land called hemp how to use a weed to make clothes and paper as well as soap and rope. This awareness allows us to build things from the baked soil and the sands of the deserts.

Children smile and offer their gratitude to the forces of energy. No slaughtering of animals to give the gods dead meat and dried up blood to transform the dead into the god called Christ. But the current matrix that rules our brains in school teaches that energy is Christ. Christ works with our western World governments and controls our thoughts or the responses to these lies. So now the majority are in line to behave. And when they do they will get the eternal reward. They can sit with this god in the afterlife. Rational thought will show you that this god is not the creator of all.

That god is the god of illusion that makes you behave so that system stays in place.

Now combining another myth let me continue. Great, we have a god but why do we follow this god. Well we need a tune. A pied piper of sorts. So now let me introduce you to the world's first troubadour. Follow me.

Osiris in this living world playing the only god needs a tune to make the people follow and obey him. To be worshiped by the people Osiris needs a melody or a virus of thought that makes you follow and flow. A flow that intoxicates and then controls you. So with the knowledge of the creator, Osiris creates Orpheus.

Then Osiris with the vibrations of love called melodies, teaches Orpheus the role he was chosen to play. Osiris puts his musical protégé on stage. This stage is required to teach man to sing and dance hearing the instruments and the motion those instruments create to get us to sway in line with the controlling thoughts of our minds.

I must add those Instruments were not for us people. No no no. Those instruments only Orpheus could play. Why? He was chosen as he had the special touch of his lips or motion of his hands those sounds gave forth the sweetness of obeying the god's wishes and wants. With this skill the motions become melodies that touch our hearts and control our minds. These earthlings are now listening to their pied piper Orpheus and his puppet master Osiris. The people are now following those vibrations to their individual ruin but to the collective combination of the whole giving their lives for the so-called god.

Osiris travels the world with his music. With love being shared with his tunes Osiris teaches mankind in the pit how to be civilized in Osiris' world order. Instead of eating what earth provides the game is changed and agriculture of food that earth did not give is created. Seeds given to the people by Osiris so what you eat keeps you depending on this god as nature knows nothing about it.

This food that civilized our world back in its day, and gave us urban order is really grains and cereals that help kill man. How? For those grains are additions to our balanced ecosystem order. Not from earth. They also are needed to domesticate the animals who eat the grains which are full of new and improved bacteria. This genetically modified food directly creates disorder and makes Illness strike man's system. But that is another story.

Now the fed earthlings living in the urban centers created by the gods, are told to work and serve their Osiris. Make your sacrifices to him and his Queen Isis. This is the priestly order of fellow mankind who serve the god. Time now for Osiris ceremonies in the Temples being built for this god. The priests spread the word. Simple command. People go to temples to bring food and animals to sacrifice to this god Osiris. If not, watch us serve you as an example to others to do as we say or else.

Do you see the connection between your stadium rockers and their traveling caravans coming to your town. You go to see your gods and you sacrifice your earnings while the gods' handlers take your coins.

In our myth in steps Typhon. The third fraternal twin of the Osiris myth of creation.

In Greek mythology we are told he was immortal. Meaning he does not die. Typhon is immune to human diseases- means he does not eat the new food. Typhon possesses superhuman strength with stamina. This Strength and Stamina skills allowed him to fight and avoid most injuries from the Olympian gods.

Typhon could also control the forces of the winds and the seas. And here he tried to control the brain disease being spread by Osiris. The lie that Osiris was the new representative of God the creator to exclusively run earth for the Creator.

Osiris who comes home to Egypt to celebrate his newfound fame falls into Typhons game. Big feast. Everybody who is anybody is there. Typhon tricks Osiris to get into a casket in front of the people, center stage, to see if the casket fits his body. Everyone at this party, banquet of the gods, was trying to get into this vampire coffin.

These gods lived off mankind's blood. That is why myths were created. Created so you believe these few were better then you so you obey and worship these few. You sanctify and magnified and give them a holy name. All so we believe they are better then we. Truth is they are not.

We were created, I repeat, to serve the few. The few who believed their role was to make us work and slave for them so they had their lifestyle here on Earth. This story of our true creation shows these aliens living here on earth were stealing the minerals of earth for their home in Nibiru. Details of this truth appear in my book called the Collonization of Earth. The Making of Mankind. A Rock Opera.

These aliens brought food, both plants and animals to earth to build urban societies. All to serve these few who called themselves gods.

So back to the creation of this myth, with Osiris in this coffin, Typhon acts quick. Typhon nails this god into the coffin. Super powers? Osiris could not get out. The prison which is what this coffin became is put into the river we call the Nile, which floats south to north.

Now when Isis learns of what happened to her fellow chess board piece, her king, she flips out. Why Isis was not at the party we are not told.. Isis appears after the deed has happened. We are told Isis cuts off a lock of her hair and puts on her mourning robes. Black robe. And now she searches the river both north and south to find the coffin.

Somehow Isis learns that the coffin ended up in the Mediterranean leaving the Nile at the Greek city we today call Alexandria. The waves take the coffin to a city then called Byblos. Byblos of the past is located about 26 miles north of Beirut. The distance of a marathon.

The coffin at first was lodged in the bushes of the tamarack tree.. But the tree grew up and swallowed the coffin.

As the myth goes, the King of this Phoenician biblical period fell in love with this gigantic tree. Ordered the tree to be cut down to be hewn into a pillar to support the roof of the Kings new palace. However the coffin was concealed in the trunk of the tree. Big tree right?

The myth says Isis heard the voice of creation. This voice told her where to go and find Osiris. Isis sits and weeps her crocodile tears at the shore next to the tamarack tree. Without Osiris, her King, she is no longer Queen.

The damsels of the Queen of Byblos hear the sighs. They appear. Bring her to the Queen who employs Isis to become the nurse of the Queens baby

Isis takes the role to be near her dead King. Isis feeds the child with her finger not her breast. Why? We are not told. But the lady is a witch as the story continues.

Isis was giving this baby the gift of immortality. She put the child every night into a fire to transform the baby into one of the gods. Isis' shape shifted into a swan so she could hover around the pillar which was now inclusive of her Kings tomb.

Queen appears and sees her baby in the fire and a swallow dancing in and out of the sun. Queen screams. The scream breaks the spell. Baby dies and Isis' shape shifts back into her human form.

In this form we are told that Isis was now surrounded with light and sweet fragrances that basically put the Queen to sleep. Isis cuts the pillar and takes the coffin with her on her broom of that day.

Isis takes the coffin to the desert. Opens it and embraces her dead king's body. Osiris was not immortal. He was just a human with a legend. A celebrity of his time.

Now the dead body must be buried where no one could find the god. Isis picks a spot in Egypt. Typhon hiding in the shadows of the moonlight sees the coffin. Grabs the coffin and opens it up.

What does Typhon do now? We are told he cuts the body up. Fourteen pieces in total. Thirteen are placed on the land. The land pieces Isis found. But the fourteenth piece was cast to the sea and never found.

In antiquity the thirteen places became places of pilgrimage. Meaning the few charged admission to be near and bear witness to the dead god called Osiris. In Egypt there are many temples to Osiris.

The fourteenth piece was Osiris' penis. Isis made an Obelisk a symbol of the missing penis and the energy that it spits in order to create and fertilize the eggs of all wombs here on earth. Isis gave it to the Egyptians to honor their dead Osiris god. The Obelisk is the Phallus that symbolizes the energy from father sun which gives the lands the energy to be fertile.

Egypt made many Obelisks for their temples to the gods. You can see one in Central Park NYC. Our US nation took it from that land. Then we placed it in Central Park Manhattan. A spot I used to run as well as bike and would always wonder why is that here. The worship of the Phallus was big in the ancient societies of mankind's time. Both in the east as well as the west. Egypt as the center point or neutral spot that divides our concept of east and west.

When Isis dies she is buried in a grave near today's Memphis Egypt. The original statue we are told had a black veil over her grave. Isis dead was more dangerous than alive.

Osiris is worshiped today around our world as the sun god in locations to this day. This myth morphed into many new names in new nations of new man-made creations This myth was needed to show the nation was created by the god of the sun. A quick rundown of the nations today who played the game telling you and all others the story of its creation.

Osiris and his many new names are listed below.

The Persians called him Mithra. The Brahms of India begin with this Sun God thought. The Phoenicians called him Baal

or Adonis. The Greeks called him Apollo. Those in Scandinavia know the energy as Odin. In Britain he was Hu. The Laplanders knew him as Baiwe.

Isis too lives on and on. She had her own witches brew in the time of Jesus, when man needed a god like figure. Isis in European lands is known as Ceres, Rhea, Venus, Venta,

Cybele, Niobe, Melissa too. Please note that the name Europe stands for the Greek goddess known as Europa. A moon goddess.

In India Isis had united a cult following. ISI, her Indian name, is the goddess of beauty as well as song and dance. The Chinese have her too immortalized as Puzza. In Britain she was once revered as Ceridwen.

Typhon had an ending too. As he had killed this first god of the creator, Zeus took him on and beat him but did not kill him. Typhon in some legends is still alive in the underworld. Typhon is the father of all monsters.

But was he?

What is truth? Why did things go the way they go? Why do we worship the living and then more so when they die? How do we create a legend and why?

This book and spoken word series is to share with others the making of a myth. And the lies needed to keep the myth alive. And boy was I involved in some of the creation as well as perpetuation of the lies that this one is better than everyone else. So time to worship this god as well as goddess amongst mankind.

I will now share with you all the creation of Ozzie "Ozzy" Osbourne and his current puppet master, queen or witch, you choose, Sharon Arden, now known as Sharon Osbourne and once known as Sharon Levy.

I wrote a book called Gods Gangsters and Honour. My English publisher gave it to Sharon to get her comments before it came out. He did not ask me. But when told I thought it would be interesting to see what happened. I told truth. I could have told much better truths but it did not fit the reason I wrote the book.

My purpose writing this book was to share the way man made gods are created. The lies and the games played to make you believe this person is better than anyone so people worship this god I represent. Worship this god or celebrity. Now, because they are a celebrity, they can sell you anything so you can be near their smell. Why? Because they are better than you. Pretty sick when you examine that truth.

Sharon needed to stop the book from being published. She was beginning her daytime talk shows. She had just finished her MTV reality TV show. A show visually sharing how sick her family was. However, for those who worship the Prince of Darkness this was cool. This sickness gave us the Kardashians and even Donald Trump. All lies so you would feel others are worse off than I am and they made it so therefore so can I.

We are so twisted we worship this perversion. Bullshit and lies. Cheats and phonies profiting off their lies as if they are the darkness that allows you to cheer up for the misery you live in. You watch this show and say thank you for what you are doing. I wish I could. Sick but welcome to mass democracy. The land of division.

The story of what happened between her and me over the then big band, Heatwave, she did not need publicized. Sharon hated black people. She did not want them around except for her maid who died in the plane crash that took out Randy Rhodes. The plane that was buzzing the bus where Sharon sat in their satanic rituals.

I wanted the truth out. Ozzie was a Don Arden creation. Don was Sharon's father. Sharon was Don's daughter whom he moved to LA and then used her domicile in LA to assist him in avoidance tax schemes when ELO became the biggest band in the world. Saying this, Don loved Sharon and there was nothing he would not give her. He just wanted her to be a lady not a rock n roller thug like him.

Me? I was the fixer. I got off on burying truths and creating lies that kept the central theme alive as I thought the means justified the end. It doesn't.

This book includes the letters of the legal battle that ensued to stop my story of Ozzy from being told of how myths are made. Hide the truth. Threaten harm either physical or through the courts, intimidate where you can, scream, curse and bribe. If not, kill the typhoon that is being thrown at you and your Isis or Osiris.

'You will see how those who get elevated status use the law and their power to hide the truth. Most are afraid to stand in truth.

I am not.

I pray this helps everyone stand in truth.

No more shadows.

Enjoy this show.

Part Two

The creation of Oz
The perpetuation of the lies

In the beginning, as the world of Ozzy was yet to be created, the English land and its people was in chaos.

All myths come from chaos. Chaos is the rule of our natural order of existence. We are a consciousness of wants and needs that come into a body to see what that individual can do in this life. Problem is we are not alone. So you fall into your parents' karma. You are born their child and that birth is marked by their slot in society before you.

As you open your eyes from your mom and dad you, by society, are pronounced a Catholic, A Jew, A Protestant and their many tribes, a Hindu, A Jain, A Buddhist. You are not labeled an Atheist which you really are at birth as you know not what you are. The trip to this body made you forget the simple truth. You are consciousness from God. You left God to have a physical life that your dreams inspired. You edge god out (EGO) and decide to become a physical god. You are baptized with your parent's label from that moment as one of us and not one of them.

Your schooling is to make you conform. Join the prison system where your dreams are put on hold until the next time. This time you will serve as a slave to the banking system that controls the currency of life. Great game. Religions are members of this elite. Governments are created as part of this elite. Bankers are created to control the spread of what you need to get to the top.

Once it was the pursuit of gold. But gold was for our makers. The gods of planet Nibiru. The planet that needed gold to keep their atmosphere in the air. This gold in liquid form was used to keep the atmosphere in place. The planet Nibiru was self-heating. So the gold keeps the heat in and keeps the heat of the sun out.

We have not seen from the Nifilim and their earth space team called the Anunnaki since the death of Alexander. We as a race were created by the Nifilim to get the gold out of the African mines and then to serve their burgeoning population of space travelers living here on earth. A planet that had the same air they breathe so they could come here and populate this planet.

This truth is in the Book of earth which I wrote. Written as a rock opera and called The Collinization of Earth. The Making of Mankind.

So to begin how was the myth of Ozzie put in rotation. And who were the initial colonizers of this dream called Ozzy?

Long time ago in our current world, 1930's in our earth time, there was a world war. The Vatican used a fool named Hitler to take over Germany and try to create a Third Reich. A Reich that would rule Europe again and force a new dark age. Yes you read right. The First Reich was when the Vatican and government appointed by the Vatican to rule the lands of Europe got together and voted in their Holy

Roman Emperor. Know this truth, the Vatican controlled the thoughts of their god Christ by manipulating earlier myths into our thoughts. Whether we agree or disagree, their story is the one we react to and therefore it controls us.

No learning. Just repeat and hear what I say. As this is the only way. No Schools of Sacred Knowledge to teach metaphysical truths. Just myths of gods and god chosen representatives like Osiris and Isis. But nature is wind and there is always someone who will appear and cause the winds of change like Typhon did in the story that begins our tale.

Now the UK was under attack because their current German King named King George VI, who ruled over the UK would not submit to Hitler's request and surrender to the Third Reich. The King would not let this Nazi force rule Europe. And Hitler's Nazi plan was that England would succumb just like the French and allow a Vichy government to rule the others while Hitler had his palace in today's West London.

Why the history? Because this is how it began. Right now the curtain rises and in this play being performed to our ancestors and future heirs in the metaphysical world we meet Harold Levy.

The Birth of a Gangster and Rock N Roll Manager

There were many German sympathizers in the UK.
The Nazis wanted to kill the Aryans that did not believe in Christ. These Aryans called themselves Jews. But they were not of Hebrew descent. No, they were of Aryan descent.

They were called Ashkenazi, which my friends, is where the word Nazi comes from.

The Nazi's whom would kill the Jews as they did not believe in the Vatican's Christ. And the Nazi's who would end the Eastern Orthodox Church as this Church did not believe the papal bulls the Vatican issued as decrees from their Christ our lord and savior.

These anti -Christ believers, Jews, had to go and so Hitler was chosen by the Vatican to kill them. If Hitler failed, which he did, the Vatican who trained their Jesuits in thought control games would bury this truth. Deny responsibility and wait to make their Fourth Reich at another earth time. The Vatican would just spread the seeds of destruction. Which they did in our lands we call the Middle East and the Balkans in our current life time.

But back to World War Two. There was an Ashkenazi, a Jew named Harold levy. Harold was born in Manchester in 1925. England had banned the Jews and only allowed the Jews back in during the 1650's after being expelled by King Edward of England in 1290.

England has the hate somewhere in their spilled blood on their earth. So the Jews then lived in fear that they would be next on Hitler's trains and stations destined to become soap and lamps or experiments to see what bacteria would do to these people when put into their system.

Harold, whom I knew as Don Arden, was hired by the underground Brits to kill Nazi sympathizers in the Manchester area. So Don told me. This is Don's beginning.

The trenches of doing anything that beasts do to stay alive so he can thrive. We are beasts. Really monkeys with a

consciousness that should know better but still falls in line and kills when fear says this is what we must do.

Remember Hitler may have been the leader but the Nazis were the Germans and Italians, French and Croatians not Siberian's or other Slavics all working hand and hand with Christ their main God.

I am a kid at heart. I love history and when Don and I would travel during my term representing him, Don would just give me stories of how he killed the Nazis for mankind. I could not get enough of it and had Don act out his first kill.

Don was proud of what he did. Don told me that this love of man he has, would never die. Don wanted to act and act he did. Harold Levy officially became Don Arden. With this change of name and his past of murder with reason in the rear view mirror Don took to the stage in Europe and played The Fiddler on the Roof.

Don tried to be-the Actor. Don did not succeed like Zero Mostel did. But Don sure tried. Don, in his stories he shared with me, was so proud that he went around Europe and proclaimed his love of Judaism.

As an Actor he relished saying 'fuck you 'to those who in the Nazi hurricane that allowed fellow men wearing the tag "Jew" to be slaughtered in public for no reason other than they could. Don did get into fights around Europe barnstorming where at the right moment, in public he would announce that the Jews survived and will now thrive. Survive another era as he barnstormed Europe in those post World War Two days.

After giving up his quest Don goes home and tries to find how he can fulfill his ambitions of perpetuating music and theatre. Back home in the UK islands Harold, now Don, gets married. But he marries a gentile. A non-Jew. Just like almost all the men who created the first government in 1946 the nation we call Israel after they survived the Nazi onslaught of European Jews.

The wife he took was named Hope Shaw. I knew her as Pat. Pat was a gentile as we just read. As Hope, before Don, she was a ballet dancer and teacher. Also, she was a woman who in time could and did control the volcanoes that lived inside Don's mind and would explode. Pat had two children if I remember right from an earlier marriage. Hidden in plain view. Don took care of them. Don took care of everyone in his family

Don, in my time with him which began in 1978, told me he was the Yiddish Godfather. I was hired with my Dad to stop the sale of United Artist records to EMI. Why? United Artists had Jet records. Dons label. Although Jet records was signed to United Artists Don was not going to EMI. Bad blood was there from before my time.

With my father Martin Machat the tales of Machat and Machat began. Dad would set the stage and I would wreck panic and fear in the hearts of these thriving corporations who look at the sale of albums as a new slot machine or better yet the first ATM machine. I knew I had to use the gun of courtroom playgrounds to scare others that their game would be exposed and I relished it.

Everyone was part of this record company retail theft. That is how you bought allegiance. And with allegiance comes the myths of why we do the things we do. It was a gangster's paradise and I thought I was the new sheriff in town. I

would protect the art of creation, not the owners, by laws of what was so created or stolen.

Don told me tales. And at our campfire late evening chats in his palatial estate in LA or London he would just drift and speak thoughts hidden in his dreams of those earlier years.

Don talked about his war with the Kray twins. See Don wanted to control the theatre of the UK. In essence become the 20th century Shakespeare. Not the myth that Shakespeare wrote the plays. No the truth. Truth is that Shakespeare was the man who said what plays will be shown. The creator of the publication of what the world will and will not know. Shakespeare in Elizabethan times was the source that approved all plays played in this Virgin Queens land.

There was trouble in the UK then known as only England. England was a name derived from an earlier word Engla-land. Engla was a miss-spelled way to say Angles. An Angles is a Germanic tribe. A tribe that settled in the UK before the Norman's took control of their seat on behalf of the Vatican's god in Britain. Britain being the name used by those who wish to convey the mystical and magical creation of this kingdom by a character known as Brutus

The Church wanted England back. And they were attacking in thoughts and war. France or Spain would start in again to bring the Pope back home to the Isles of Britain. Ireland stayed catholic and the war between the Church of Rome or the English Church still breathes today.

Catholic religion did invade England. We are not taught this truth but they did. That invasion happened in 1066. September 28th to be exact in a place called Battle but we are told it was called Hastings. Two towns near each other.

1066 my friends is also the year that the Church finally separated into two. Each side excommunicated each other. The Western Church and the Vatican who said Jesus was Christ and this is how we control you. The Eastern Church ran in the Greek lands then known as Constantine who believed in the metaphysical Jesus Christ. The essence of love not control.

England was the land of mystery and myths. The English believe these myths as it gives them a reason to be. These myths create new creations as the real dreamers, known as creators, can create in those islands. And so we will now continue our tale.

Robin Hood and Arthur the King fought the rules of wrong order and control. They were gangsters. So England was raised on myths of those who fought the then law and order. So after World War Two, in this war, the nation's gangsters or warlords appear and this story now turns to the Creation of the Kray Twins

The Kray twins were a curious duo. They were killers. Wikipedia says the twin brothers " were English criminals, the foremost perpetrators of organized crime in the East End of London during the 1950's and 1960's. With their gang known as "The Firm", the Kray's were involved in murder, armed robbery, arson, protection rackets and assaults. "

In the 1960's, the Kray twins ran the nightclubs of London and the suburban world. They were branching out. They got involved in entertainment. And entertainment needed their own gangsters to stop the spread of Krayism.

So skipping through the time let's move to the 60's.

England, now really promoting the god of Orpheus, was creating music heard around the world. The English invasion soon to be called the British Invasion. Again, Britain being a name given, after Brutus in the myth of creation, to the British Isles. This British music invasion covered the Welch and the Scots as well as the Irish. Even some transplanted Brits living in Australia set their sights on the center stage of the war baby generation.

These nations feed off myths. So does religions. So does the creation of new gods and goddesses and their gangsters to make you follow the tunes of the latest pied piper.

So now Music is in the air and every creation needs a gangster of some sort to perpetuate the myths of ownership and control of your mind.

England the land, the United Kingdom the nation needed gangsters to stop the Kray twins and their creation of thought control with tribute to the landlords of the clubs and retail businesses. Protection from crimes. These gangsters start and end when you agree to pay them protection. A new church who shows you how you will be killed until you submit to their land rules of everything you do.

Don goes into business with two other gangsters in their own right. A federated church of sorts. Each had their own fiefdom but they would rally to support each other. We now have a three headed organization that would protect you the artist from organized crime by others.

The first new teammate with Don is a man we today know as Peter Grant. Peter was an Englishman. We know him as the manager of Led Zeppelin from their beginning. That beginning was 1968 when the Kray's were arrested and taken off the streets.

Wikipedia says Grant was born and largely brought up in the south London suburb of South Norwood. He was born before the War of 1939. This south London area was bombed by the Germans and their Luftwaffe. Today the German number one airplane fighter is known as Eurofighter Typhoon. Typhoon the destroyer in myths of others' creations.

Grant grew up learning to survive. Without a father, Peter was a bit part actor by heart. But his trade was to survive. So to survive he needed to be paid. His trade was being a stagehand as well as a thug. A thug who played bouncer and protector of others' properties. Both possessions and people.

Don knew Peter. In fact two bands that Don managed while Sharon was in her teen years the Animals and Small faces Don had hired Peter to be the tour manager. Well really the enforcer. As Don told me there were a few setbacks in his civil being. Like taking Robert Stigwood, Bees Gees fame, with some enforcers out of his office and then holding him over the ledge of his patio until Stigwood agreed to leave Don's acts alone. The act was the Animals who were

managed by Don and produced by Mickie Most. Most is whom Dad was the lawyer for in those British Invasion days. It is where the Machat's story with Arden begins.

Dad was scared of Don the legend. He stayed clear.

I asked Don how he could do that to Stigwood. Don said he had to. His reputation was at stake and he did not want anyone poaching his acts. I said but to take the man out of the office and hold him over the balcony how could you be part of that? His answer to me was the enforcers got carried away. And lucky they did not drop him. And Don adds it was only the second floor.

By the way, who was in charge of these enforces- Peter Grant. As in those days bands were taken from their ownership deals by other managers all the time.

Sharon was in awe of dad the thug. David the son as I got to know him was embarrassed. Very embarrassed. Sharon lived her days as a thug. Copying dad. Dad was the teacher. But dad did not want Sharon in this business as we shall learn.

Gangster two was a man named Patrick Meehan. Patrick was another enforcer used by Don in his 60's anti Kray controlled days.

Patrick was ready to branch out with his own company around 1970. Patrick got the management and control of Black Sabbath. This band was originally signed to a club promoter from Birmingham England named Jim Simpson. Birmingham was the place of birth for Black Sabbath. Don had the band the Move who were from this region. The Move blossomed into ELO.

Don's tentacles with Grant and Meehan, controlled this area when the aspiring artists thought they were ready for London town. When Don got near the others trying to get their piece of the new talent with Don in the air, others knew a fight would ensue. Some bowed out. Simpson was history. Simpson did however lead the band to their first platform of success.

This group of lads begin with the album Black Sabbath. Then came Paranoid. This album was when this creation was discovered by the mass media. The energy of these four created a methodical beat with Ozzy's haunting lyrics at times to make you feel you were part of the Black Sabbath ritual. Howling at the moon to get a new sun to come and save your day.

Black Sabbath being the worship of the other side.

Yes witchcraft. Turn others' light of control which we are told is light to be seen for what it is. It is darkness. All worship is darkness as it shuts out your ability to see lights of other truths in a universe where there are many truths depending on what you are seeing and what you see through the prisms of your mind as opposed to the rhythms of your heart.

Worship of all things and places and not yourself with God, that is witchcraft. At the Black Sabbath's, your controlled light is now darkened by the thoughts that loosen the particles of energy inside your thick head, called quantum physics, and the control of your mind is set free. You now can and probably do and follow the tunes that this pied piper in black, the Isis or Typhon from outside your matrix is enticing you to join.

So the band back then called Black Sabbath were comprised of four lads. First was drummer Bill Ward. Second in alphabetical order as if this is Apple Music is bassist Geezer Butler. Third is vocalist the lad forever now known as Ozzy Osbourne and fourth was guitarist Tony Iommi.

Sharon knew this band from the beginning. Sharon and David were taught to discover who was happening in club lands around the Isles so Don could get them to join his kingdom.

The Sabbath quartet were then kids. Patrick gave them success at the helm. The band was controversial amid claims they were not and would not be part of the material world. They lied. It was always about the money. How you could bend time and create the space for you to join the orbit of controlling thoughts in the matrix of our lives. A new band needs to convince others they are not the same as what you presently have. So follow me and we will discover what can be as I sing you a tune that you will pay me to share and help you get to your new space here on this living earth.

Nothing new. No matter what we do.

Now Grant gets Zeppelin. Meehan has Black Sabbath and Don has the Move. The Move led by Roy Wood and going nowhere.

Grant leaves first. Now it is Don and Patrick. But as in all relationships money gets in the way and the two split. This break up is not good. The kids of these two were friends and grew up together. But the papa's went to war. They have the famous brawl in the music industry's convention called Midem, which then was to showcase your acts. Today it is to sell your business of others' creations. Acts today do not matter only the song remains the same. No need for more legends. Stadium acts are done. Today it is the festival that counts. Things change and so will this. But that's later.

Don and Patrick had real bad blood. Revenge was the name of Dons game. Don knew he would get his chance and wait he did. Meehan lost the act in 75 but kept the publishing and a piece of the record royalties. Don wanted revenge and it came in 1979.

Don had ELO and that's where I enter the game. I am the son of a man who was the lawyer that would threaten the labels on behalf of the managers to get more money. Dad did this. But dad was in touch with the artists who loved dad and could get the companies to pay more than they originally agreed to pay. Dad taught me this game well. And dad taught me to have no fear.

Dad wanted me to be his gangster and clean up the messes that would occur when our company Machat and Machat rode into town.

I relished the position. I was young. And this position kept me in touch with creation. Allowed me to travel the world. Learn truths and understand the creation of myths.

I was then a fixer, a myth maker, a bard and now a seeker of truth. Looking for justice so we all can live a dream and stop believing others are better than we are.

So for those who wish to pursue a career in arts you must understand this truth. You the artist wanted to be the new creation and to get there you needed a gangster to perpetuate the lie and make others believe you were the new Jesus Christ.

And my friends, I knew and know this game. I know the game and watched it being played as well as played it. I did it with my son Barron and it took his life as this evil Black Sabbath we called Lean created an energy of devil worship that my son fell into and he is gone captured in that storm of a blood ritual taking place in my apartment the night my son fled my flat in Miami in fear that's this black cloud would do him harm.

Watch out for what you do. Every action has a reaction and it's not always what you believe it will be. You see what is going on. Now with a virus that mankind created that escaped its petri origins and got into our atmosphere and reproduced and took our lives living here on earth.

So now let's go to 1979. I meet Black Sabbath and get them to agree to do what Don wants me to do. Fire the labels that Meehan still gets his piece of the royalties on Sabbath sales and make them a deal where Don gets his piece.

I thought I was building an empire.

I am running the business called Jet Records. Overseen by their god Don Arden. Two main offices. One in London and one in LA. I was in charge of LA which was helmed by Sharon and Dad was in charge of London helmed by Don's son David. I reported to Don as did Dad. Dad was Dad and he humored Don looking to see if there was money for him in it. I was looking to build an empire of creation. To create, it takes is more than money. You need talent.

Don and I bonded. I loved his tenacity and his fight to build his family no matter what their flaws were. Don and Dad were my gurus. Soon I will get others too. Neither of them were metaphysical. I always was. And those two taught me this physical game of chasing the golden yellow path of money.

At the same time I must admit I admire how Sharon bull dozed her way into becoming a woman of voice and respect by the few who profit off her celebrity hood.

Now the book deals with Ozzy, Sharon, Me and Don. You will read the chapters as they were originally written to share the creation of Ozzy. First up are the original chapters in my book Gods Gangsters and Honor. Then comes the lawyers' letters to try and stop the book from publication. My publishers' responses follow. And as a tennis game then their response and ours.

After this series of letters you will see how truths are converted to lies with truths in the middle but coated so you believe in the new myths of creation. Today's world of celebrityhood. You see how it is done.

I end this book with the revised chapters with my point still there but Sharon's major complaints taken out which I told everyone involved I would publish these truths and now I do.

The book ends with how I consigned myself to live with honor in my own truth. If Sharon did not fight me I do not know if I would be the man I became.

So I thank you Ms. Sharon Levy.

And to all who read this I will confess I do admire how you became what you are today. You took your role as the daughter of a gangster and then a supportive Queen and launched out your own world without anyone at helm but yourself .

I salute you. Know that because to overcome your past and bury it was not easy to do. That is the myth that must be taught. Very inspiring. How you overcame those truths to be the woman today people see and feel.

Love or hate you make people believe in something more than just the routine they are mired in every day.

Know that your mom and dad are proud of you.

Don Arden

Don Arden's
First Single

Coronation of King George VI

Ozzy Osbourne
Arrest Photo

The Killer Krays

Isis

Osiris

Horus

Ozzy in
Black Sabbath

Peter
Grant

Robert
Stigwood

Orpheus

Pope
Innocent
VIII

Small
Faces

Pope Innocent VIII teaches the church
how to identify a witch

The following section contains first the unedited, chapters from Steven Machat's book, "Gods, Gangsters and Honour", which the Osbournes contested with legal intimidation in order to bury the truths and perpetuate lies.

These chapters are followed by legal exhibits documenting the involved dispute by the Osbournes with Steven Machat.

Machat himself was not threatened by the Osbournes. The Osbournes attempted to threaten the publisher so the publisher would not print the book. But Steven Machat's desire to live his truths prevailed and the book was published.

He is sharing this you so that you can see how celebrities create lies and new myths by intimating those who dare to speak the truth.

CHAPTER EIGHTEEN

Who's afraid of Don Arden?

We were ready to sign the biggest deal in the history of the music business and there was Sharon Arden's Yorkie dog peeing under the desk of Myron Roth – then one of the most powerful record executives in the world.

To make matters worse Sharon was crying with laughter, as the dog peed amid the splendour of the Beverly Hills office of CBS, the world's biggest record label.

But what shocked me most of all was that Roth did nothing. At stake was the world's biggest band and a US$50 million deal and when that kind of money is at stake its shit-eating grins all round.

The date was 12th May 1978 and my father Marty Machat, Sharon Arden (now, of course, better known as Sharon Osbourne), Myron Roth, who was the head of CBS Records on the West Coast, and myself had convened for a signing at Roth's office. We were there to sign the contracts for the Electric Light Orchestra, which was owned and managed by Jet Records, a Delaware company owned and run with an iron fist by Sharon's father, Don Arden.

My father and I, who were the lawyers for Jet, had brokered the deal with CBS and Sharon was Don's signing representative in the US because her father was in tax exile on both sides of the Atlantic.

Inevitably, there was a delay as the contracts were being copied and Sharon was playing the Spoiled Princess as usual, making it clear that she was very bored at being kept waiting. As Roth disappeared for the umpteenth time, it became clear that Sharon's white toy dog could hold on no longer, so it ended up under the desk where it took its leak. My poker face came in handy, but I was dying inside because I could see $50 million going down the pan. My father's jaw went slack, but Sharon just laughed as Roth's rug became a dog's toilet.

When Roth walked back into the room his face dropped through the floor. 'What the fuck is this?' Roth asked. Sharon fixed him with a laser glare: 'It's dog wee, you fool,' she said in her little girl's voice. 'What do you think it is?'

If he'd had any self respect, Roth would have thrown Sharon out there and then, but there was too much money at stake and he knew it. As he stalked out, Sharon caught my eye and said, 'Wait until he finds out the dog has peed over there too.'

The contracts were duly signed on Roth's desk. The aroma of the urine hung in the air.

When I first came across the Ardens in September 1977 my dad warned me to steer clear of them, but I'm afraid that only sparked my interest.

I'd had a call from a Canadian one-hit wonder called JJ Barrie, while I was sat in my father's office on 22 Dean Street, in the heart of London's Soho. Barrie, who specialised in slushy and sentimental tunes, thought that he was about to get a deal with Jet and David Arden, Don's only son. (Don Arden was born Don Levy but changed his name to Arden as he started in the business after WWII and thought the name Levy would hold him back.)

Barrie thought I could represent him in his impending meeting with David Arden, but my father was not impressed with either Barrie or the Ardens.

'Forget it. Barrie is a waste of time and space and the Ardens are dangerous and full of shit. It always ends up in nothing. Don't touch 'em.'

My father had had a flirtation with Don Arden a few years back, but after this went nowhere he was once bitten, twice shy. Known as the English gangster of pop, Arden had a reputation for violence, intimidation and sharp practice that got my creative juices going. I had to find out more. In fact, the more my father dragged up the stories about Don Arden, the more I was hooked, and I decided to persuade my father to green-light our involvement with Barrie.

From the moment that I got to meet David Arden, it was embarrassingly obvious that Jet had no interest in Barrie. What was also obvious, was that the sons of Machat Senior and Arden Senior were sizing one another up, with an eye on future business deals. Poor Barrie could only watch on.

David and I agreed to meet for dinner in the Chelsea Rendezvous, a chic restaurant in Sydney Street where at the time pop rockers would dine. As David, his wife Jane, and I sat drinking, eating and chewing the fat, we realised that there must be something in the air because our neighbours, four Arabs dressed up in full robes, were calling David a 'poofter'.

I realised this was a chance to make an impression on Don Arden's son, and therefore Don. I instinctively did something I have never done before or since: I challenged the Arabs to a fight, after pushing the table over them and showering them with abuse. Our reward was that we were thrown out of the restaurant.

News of the altercation must have reached Don because later that month, he called Dad up and offered Machat and Machat the chance to work with him. It was a deal so big that Dad managed to overcome his scruples about the Ardens, and we were in.

The deal was perfect. I would pair up with Don on the West Coast, while my father and David Arden would hold the fort in London. The first major task we were handed in 1978 was to broker new deals for Don's label Jet and his number one act: the Electric Light Orchestra.

Their seventh studio album *Out of the Blue* had hit paydirt, reaching number 4 in the album charts on both sides of the Atlantic but more importantly staying inside the Top 20 for a

good year and a half. The singles *Sweet Talking Woman* and
Mr Blue Sky were both Top 10 hits and the public's appetite
for their mix of classical and pop rock was growing.

The CBS contracts that we signed for ELO and other Jet
artists in May 1978 were masterpieces. In their own way they
were every bit as good as a Beethoven score, Shakespeare manuscript, or Picasso canvas. They would revolutionise the music
business and secure the reputation globally of both Don Arden
and his company Jet, and also establish the Machats as world-
class, contemporary, business-savvy operators. Dad was no longer
yesterday's man.

For the US and Canada, the ELO deal was worth $35 million
up front, which included $17 million to pay off United Artists
who had a stake in ELO. In addition, Jet Records received a
basic $6m an album and any subsequent albums would see the
advance rise provided sales of the preceeding album had met
agreed targets.

For the rest of the world we made two seperate deals with
CBS. Outside the US, Canada and the UK, we got $10 million
per album. For brokering all these deals, the Machats got an
upfront fee of $750,000. The second deal was for the UK and
Eire. It represented the pinnacle of my father's career and reflected
his genius as a deal maker. Jet became a mainstream record label
funded by CBS and Jet had complete freedom to sign and supply
whatever artist they wanted for that jurisdiction. CBS had to
pay the promoting, marketing and manufacturing costs and had
to pay £20,000 per month to Jet for five years for general
expenses. I wrote into the contract that the Machats would get
£5,000 a month of the £20,000 that CBS were contracted to
give Jet every month. I never wanted to ask or chase the Ardens
for our share.

By any measure, this was a lot of money. We had earned our
keep with a record royalty deal for the band. Even better, our
contract would bootstrap ELO to this record high royalty rate
across the CBS world. If anyone offered a better deal our contract

would match that deal.

But what was truly revolutionary about all this was that there were two groups of contracts, and this detail helps explain the unique nature of the deal we had secured. Forgive the business discussion, but the devil – and the truth – is in the detail.

The first contract was between the Arden clan's Jet Records and CBS and the second was between CBS, Jet and ELO. The reasons for this are both simple and complex and to understand why is to appreciate why the music business is an accountant's main course.

Let's say I am an up-and-coming band with a lawyer representing us and we are approached by the biggest label in the world – and believe you me, at that time CBS was the biggest.

The band and the manager lay it on the line: we want the lot. Drugs, girls, hookers, cocaine, houses, hedge fund account and so on. So CBS tease and taunt for a short while, but eventually the offer comes through: we'll give you everything you want. At the same time, CBS would offer the management a second deal: a co-production deal for other artists.

Brilliant? Well no. Because the record labels cross-collateralise against everything. Cross what? Well, it's simple really. CBS will deal with you – the artist's manager and your production company – as long as you have a hit band. They will flatter your ego and encourage you to put out records by other bands you manage.

Let's say those other bands flop and flop some more. They almost always do. Well, all losses incurred by those 'loser' bands will be set against your one hit band. Pretty soon, you could even find yourself owing money to the label and unable to pay your one successful band.

Further, the label will encourage you to put out records by your other bands on their labels because they add up the figures. They alone can then manipulate the bottom line so that you end up looking like a complete and utter failure. But the label itself makes money.

CBS had to approve all subsequent contracts that Jet signed with artists if they were to be released on Jet/CBS in the United States – but not if they were released in the UK. So all I did was write contracts that CBS could not approve, because Jet was losing too much money and we could not afford any flop bands.

The cute thing about the ELO deal was that the risk was all left at the door of CBS. No-one in the business could believe that we had done it. As far as I know, it was a first and made people in the industry really sit up and take notice.

But Arden and his clan were about to learn some bitter lessons. So were we. From the moment they signed the ELO deal, Jet could not buy another hit act – literally. Try as hard as they might, Jet were haemorrhaging red ink. They had one miss after another and CBS was apparently happy to let this situation carry on.

Eventually, Jet's roster became an open joke in the industry. ELO was paying for Jet's losses, even if they were not set against the band by CBS.

CBS bigwig Walter Yetnikoff called a pow-wow. He had an offer: Jet could have the band Journey. My eyes lit up because Journey were a hit band. Set up by various Santana alumni, Journey would, like ELO, develop into essentially a label and management conceit. Members of Journey would come and go largely at the whim of the band's management and label suits who were really only interested in the bottom line. Art was going out of the window. Music was becoming nothing more than a box of cereal. This was the way music was going, but the public clearly didn't care because by the early 1980s Journey was a corporate rock band designed to sell records, with huge-selling hit albums under their belt and top ten hits galore. Yetnikoff was doing this often without any input from Journey or their management. Remember, he thought he was a God.

So we set up a meeting during the summer 1978 tour of ELO

but from the start, Sharon made it clear that she would have nothing to do with the band. She said: 'Journey's fuckin' bullshit. They'll never sell anywhere near ELO and Jet will have nothing to do with them.'

Sharon let the people at Journey know what she thought of them. She knew damn well that once Journey knew she had a problem with them, they would have a problem with Jet. They would have nothing to do with Sharon. Because Sharon was Don Arden's representative for the US, she could veto anything and everything that she didn't like or want until Don returned. As Don told me: 'Sharon watches LA while I'm not there. I love her and would trust her with my life. She's got my balls and guts but she can't run the business. This is a man's business.'

So Jet lost out on Journey, and continued to lose money time and time again. Like when, in August 1978, the Electric Light Orchestra played Pontiac in Michigan, in what was fast turning into the most successful rock tour ever. Sharon was the label's representative on the road.

Called *The Big Night*, the nine-month ELO tour revolutionised rock performances thanks to its monumentally huge set and a fantastically expensive spaceship stage with fog and lasers. At the Cleveland Stadium alone, around 80,000 people watched ELO and the tour broke all rock records with its grosses at the Anaheim show, which pulled in $5 million.

But ticket sales for the Michegan show were looking poor, and the local promoter, Brass Ring, tried to re-negotiate its deal with Jet to cover its losses.

The costs of running the show were sky-high and Jet couldn't afford to re-negotiate, so they turned down their plea flat. To be fair, if the show had sold out, the promoters would have made a killing and would never have offered to share the windfall. So why reduce the risk?

Brass Ring retaliated by threatening non-payment of the monies due to Jet on the existing ticket sales, and this presented real problems because Jet were performing a financial high-wire act. The tour was expensive to run and we needed the money to pay the road cost. This was tit-for-tat. We threatened to pull ELO. Brass Ring turned around and offered a cashier's cheque, but as Jet's brain I knew they couldn't be trusted.

It was a trick I'd learned about in studying for my bar exams. The promoters give you the cheque just before the show, the show goes ahead and by the time you bank it, they've cancelled the cheque.

Eventually a compromise was reached: they would give us a cheque with enough time to cash it ahead of the show.

Inevitably, Brass Ring kept us waiting until Friday afternoon, after the end of bank hours, which then would have 3pm local time, and by then it was too late (banks only worked Monday to Friday in those days). First thing Monday, the cheque was cancelled.

I urged Jet to cancel the show, because it was obvious by that point that we were going to get screwed. But nobody listened to me. So on Saturday, it went ahead and come Monday, we had a problem.

Don Arden flipped out. He threatened to kill all sorts of people, and threatened all kinds of retribution on the promoters. We filed a lawsuit in Michigan – but Brass Ring had an ace up its sleeve. They claimed that they and the public had been defrauded because Brass Ring had been given to believe that ELO were a live act when they were not. They claimed that most of the show was actually pre-recorded or taped. They had taken a gamble that ELO mastermind Jeff Lynne would shy away from litigation, because the truth that ELO had pre-recorded most of their material would be very embarrassing if it came out in court.

Brass Ring was right, Jeff Lynne would not testify and they got away with it. If proof were needed, the Michigan farce gave plenty of evidence that ELO was not all it seemed. In reality, a lot of their stage act did indeed rely on tapes.

The truth was that ELO were as much a creation of Don

Arden as they were Jeff Lynne. The stage show that projected ELO into global stardom was the brainchild of Don Arden. Not Sharon. Not Jeff Lynne. Just Don.

What ELO and Arden did was revolutionise stage shows. Not just with their pyrotechnics, lasers and lights, but also by the use of tapes. After ELO, you saw other big bands like Pink Floyd go on the road and increasingly rely on pre-recorded material to create the kind of aural impact that sold out tours.

Nowadays the use of tapes in live acts is common place. Look at Madonna and her shows, for instance: there is no human alive who could perform those stage routines and keep up live singing, as she appears to do.

For these reasons if no other, ELO and Don Arden had helped shape the future direction of corporate rock. I often think that Don doesn't really get the credit he deserves on this front, for all his alleged faults.

Although I idealised Don Arden, and as much as he was a surrogate father figure, I had no illusions about the true measure of the man. I knew he was a man.

Remember, this is the man who introduced me to the woman who would become my wife and got us first-class tickets to Tahiti for our wedding and honeymoon. Don treated me and Lisa by way of his travel agent Howard Sinclair, who was based in the UK but had an office in LA. We figured this was a nice gift.

Then a year later the federal authorities came a-calling. They wanted to know how I got the tickets, how much I paid for them, and so on. Why? Because it turned out, the tickets were stolen. Don had given me stolen tickets, which his agent charged him for.

Don was always trying something on. I remember going along to an office meeting at Jet in London in 1978. Suddenly all these people were shouting at me. Apparently I had been abusing the company expense account.

Don had been booking me in at the London hotel, the Montcalm, for the weekend before my actual arrival, on my visits to the UK. I was dumbstruck. I kept looking at Don but he made a hand sign to indicate that I was on my own on this one. He knew I would be able to take the heat.

When Don left the room, I cornered him and he said: 'Sorry kid, but I had to leave that well alone.' It turned out that he had been using the hotel suite on Friday and Saturday nights under my name so he could see his mistress without using his own name. Then he'd put me in a single room. Because I only ever arrived on Sundays it was the perfect cover for his dalliances.

Don's greatest flaw, however, was not the bullshit or the crooked stuff. That went with the territory – this was the entertainment industry, after all.

The real problems lay with Don's extravagance. Nothing lasts forever. We humans forget that as you rise to the top, gravity still applies: what goes up will come down.

Take ELO's Anaheim Stadium show in 1978. It grossed a then world record $5 million, but Don managed to make a $500,000 loss on it. The reason was that he was determined to make a lasting impression on the entertainment business, so he paid for a spectacular laser show in the sky above the concert.

This cost Jet an absolute fortune. Then, for the after show party, he insisted on everyone drinking Cristal champagne, which was ridiculously expensive and, worse, being downed by 500 people.

My father, always the armchair quarterback, said: 'Don is so dumb. After the first glass, no-one can taste the difference. He shoulda switched to Spanish champagne.'

But Don believed that you had to create this image to make it in LA and he had a point.

For all this, however, there was no greater extravagance than his daughter, and the image she created was precious little credit to Don or Jet.

Don indulged and spoiled her and created untold problems for himself in the process. Sharon repaid her father's indulgence cruelly.

Throughout my time with Jet it was clear that she held a grudge. She believed that she had good reasons for despising her father and her brother.

I can well remember going to the Arden's lavish Christmas party at the Beverly Hilton Hotel in Christmas 1978. This was intended to mark their arrival as global players and also signal to the industry that they were here to stay.

No expense was spared, and when you walked into the hotel there was a big display: 'Don and David Arden and Jet Records welcomes you.' There was no mention of Sharon.

I was in the reception area when Sharon swanned in like she owned the joint. The look on her face when she saw that display stays with me. You could tell that horror, fury and humiliation embossed her ego there and then. She believed she was the LA boss – the banner confirmed she was not.

Just so Sharon got the message, this also happened at Jet's London party that same Christmas.

As the son and heir of the Arden's empire, it was David who got the credit and respect for the success of ELO. The glory that should have been afforded to Don's daughter, Sharon. At least that was the way Sharon saw it. But if her father was not going to give her the credit that she was due, then Sharon would go it alone.

Sharon spent and spent. By the end of the decade, Jet were out of money and in 1981 I would be selling off Jet's ELO publishing rights to raise money for the creaking Arden empire. It's possible that Sharon believed that by spending Jet's money, she could bring Don to his knees and beg her to help him out.

In 1979, I had to block Sharon after she tried to buy a convertible Mercedes for one of her many would-be lays. What made this worse, was that the recipient was William Mamone, who only five years earlier had beaten the shit out of Don Arden. Mamone had been working for Don and his associates, Patrick Meehan Senior and Peter Grant – the Holy Gangster Trio of British management. William left when Meehan set up his own business managing Black Sabbath and others; and Peter Grant left when he took over a guitar player called Jimmy Page with a singer called Robert Plant from the Band of Joy, and created Led Zeppelin.

Meehan had worked with Arden for years, but after splitting to set up his own business, the pair had fallen out big time over money and a full-on feud developed. Meehan wanted Arden to pay him back £5,000 which he had lent him in lean times. Arden told him to 'fuck off'. When the warring parties met in Cannes in 1974 at the MIDEM fair, a huge fight ensued with broken tables galore, wounded guests and, for once, Don found himself on the receiving end. Mamone had decided that the best way to defend his honour was to give Don a taste of his own medicine, and he gave Don a thorough beating. Sharon got a smack in the face for her troubles during the ensuing medley of bodies.

But when Sharon bumped into Mamone in 1979, she decided to get up close and personal with her father's arch enemy and, in order to induce future favours, decided to try to reward him with the car.

Mamone told me only this year that he never fell for Sharon's charms. He also told me that she unfastened his pants quicker than anyone.

I blocked the transaction, which didn't improve my relationship with Sharon, although in truth we largely got on because we had to. We had offices in the same building at Jet, and knew the same people. One of their records promotion men used to do drugs in Sharon's office, and afterwards would come up to my office and share his blow with me. He had some mouth on him. He couldn't resist gossip and I got to learn about all of Sharon's latest indiscretions if I hadn't heard them from Don already.

By 1980 my father wanted me back in New York and out of Jet and the Ardens, but truth be told, I was by then addicted to Don. I could not and would not walk away from Don.

The straw that broke the camel's back for my father was when Jeff Lynne claimed Don was ripping him off and was therefore in breach of contract. This was way too much work for Dad. He said no, but I said, we'll fix this.

This contract was my coming of age.

Lynne, who was terrified of Don, was desperately trying to get out of his Jet contract. Don Arden wanted me to redraw the contracts to keep Lynne on board and CBS were happy to underwrite this because they did not want to lose one of their hottest artists.

During one of the preliminary meetings, I met up with Don and Jeff Lynne's new lawyer in Cannes, where Lynne had moved with his new wife for the summer holidays. I set about wooing one of Lynne's lawyers. I had to, to get the deal done. It was pretty simple really: I got him to close the deal while we were snorting blow together and discussing his nightmare marriage.

I persuaded the lawyer to write into the contract $500,000 direct from CBS so he would not have to seek Lynne's payment after the fact. I told him, and he listened, that he should tell CBS that this was the only way to secure the contract. I figured I was worth at least half, so I scooped $250,000.

Eventually everything was lined up, except the new contracts from CBS: since they were putting the money up, they could draft the contracts. The negotiators told me that they would stay up all night to draft the contracts, on condition that I scored them large amounts of blow, which I did. They stayed up all night, and I can see their faces lined with shit-eating grins and glazed eyes when I walked into their offices at 9am the next morning.

I even loaned my flat to the lawyer that evening so he could entertain his mistress, who he later married, and did my best to make sure he had a good time. I didn't want him staying at CBS overseeing the contracts. My plan was that he would be too tired the following day to pay close attention to the contractual clauses. That way he would make mistakes and I would be in control.

Call me cynical, but by the time everyone walked into the CBS boardroom everything was ready to go. But there was one problem.

Lynne had turned up with another attorney, an English tax attorney named Sam Sylvester, and when this attorney started reading through the inducement clauses, and explained them to Lynne, the ELO leader went a deathly pale and broke out into a cold sweat. Jeff too was using a tax shelter production company, but CBS required an inducement letter. The inducement letter is basically a letter that confirms that the individual is bound to the production company and will only look to the production company for the money, not CBS.

Everyone was terrified the deal was about to go south. What was the problem? The problem was the insurance clause that said that in event of Lynne dying, Don got the insurance pay-off.

Lynne was convinced that this would encourage Don to kill him off. Only when the clause was altered, so that CBS became the beneficiaries, would Lynne finally sign on the dotted line.

Everybody was scared of Don Arden. But me, I just understood his show.

CHAPTER TWENTY-SIX

The birth of the Queen of Hearts

Sharon Osbourne said she had $500,000 in her handbag and was determined to make me an offer. Leaning over my desk and with her green eyes trying to laser a hole through me, she was every bit as blunt as her father Don Arden when riled, and just as charmless.

It was 1984 and Sharon was talking about the contract of her new husband, Ozzy Osbourne. It looked like the real life version of Lewis Carrol's Queen of Hearts was proposing to buy out my interest.

She said: 'Steven, I've got half a million dollars in cash in this briefcase. Just give me all the books and records about Ozzy, including the Princess Productions corporation stuff and Jet Records shit. You don't need to be involved again.'

Tempting as this offer was, I didn't trust Sharon and besides, I wasn't prepared to sell out my business partner, guiding light and surrogate father Don Arden.

In any event, I didn't believe the case had $500,000 in it: more likely $50,000, if that. Knowing Sharon as well as I did, she would have spent the rest.

'Get the fuck out of my office. I'm not getting in the middle of a family feud,' I replied.

This just made matters a whole lot worse. Sharon could never take no for an answer and she decided I should hear some home truths, even if they weren't true, had nothing to do with my home and I didn't want to listen.

'You're a moron. Always have been and always will be. There isn't a family feud. How can there be? My Dad is already dead. Take the fucking money now or you're going to get fuck all.'

I decided it was time to give as good as I got because my

courtesy was getting me nowhere: 'Sharon, please, go and fuck yourself. You'll get the books over my dead body, which, in case you get any ideas, ain't going to happen any time soon. It's about time you grew up and it's about time you kissed and made up with your Dad. He doesn't deserve this.'

Then Sharon decided to analyse my marriage and wife in language that would shame someone with Tourettes syndrome. She said: 'Are you some kind of fucking moron? Your wife is a retard and it's about time you wised up. I bought your wife by hiring the LA Rams cheerleaders to appear at the Jet CBS party at my house where you met your dream – so fuck you.'

At that point, I noticed that my father was at the door and Machat Senior told me I should sign on the dotted line. The inference was clear: 'Take the cash and just get rid of the bitch'. My Dad was convinced that Sharon wasn't worth the hassle and I should cut a deal. But I wasn't having it, because it was getting way too personal and my loyalties lay with Don Arden.

'Dad, when David Puttnam tried to poach me and all those other job offers came my way, you were upset. We're a family business, regardless of what shit is going down. You always told me you wouldn't want anyone interfering in the family business and so why should we be bought by one side of the Ardens or the other?'

I didn't want to get drawn into a feud that had run long and bitter. My father turned around to Sharon and said: 'Unfortunately, Steven is right. I wish I didn't have to say that, but he is right.' Not exactly a ringing vote of confidence but at least I had won the argument at Machat and Machat.

As Sharon left she screamed: 'My Dad is a piece of shit. He will fuck your life when he needs to.'

With a few deafening exceptions, I would not hear the wrath of Sharon again until 1999. I would discover that her thought processes and vocabulary had not improved in the intervening years.

Legend has it that Don handed Ozzy's contract to Sharon as a wedding gift. But he only gave Sharon the managing contract, which was only one part of his contractual equation with Ozzy, and a modest one at that.

Don kept the publishing and production contracts. He thought he knew exactly what he was doing, but he hadn't banked on Sharon's ruthlessness. His gesture of convenience would rebound on Don horribly.

By keeping the production and publishing contracts, the Ardens could earn off Ozzy twice over and with no ethical problems – not that ethics were ever a particular issue with that family.

As a manager, you're supposed to keep an eye on everything involving your artist, not least the publishers, record labels and producers, to make sure they don't screw your artist. Those relationships aren't meant to be held by the same party, but they can be. Each relationship is special and the general rules are for fools. You just have to work out what is best.

If you own both sides of the same coin, there's an obvious conflict of interest. Because Don and Sharon were no longer in business together, there was no potential conflict of interest between the artist and the agreements, so long as each did their best.

And by giving Sharon the management contract, this meant that Don kept the real money-spinners that lay in publishing and production – the publishers and production companies get paid first – but got Sharon off his back and Ozzy too, as Sharon had control of the tour income and the merchandising income, which was big. The key to any contract is who holds the exclusive administration rights. You get paid first and thereby you have control.

Now Sharon would be able to receive Ozzy's commissions on merchandising and touring.

But rather than thanking her father, Sharon turned around and sued him for all he was worth, claiming that Don had been not been accounting the royalties due to Ozzy as well as the rest of the band members, the men who really wrote and created the Blizzard of Oz. Clearly, she was her father's daughter after all.

This legal action would ensure that daughter and father would remain estranged for more than 15 years. It didn't help that all the Jet parties shared the same accountant: Colin Newman.

Ironically enough, only my involvement and another bitter and twisted law suit more than a decade later would bring them back together again.

There are so many layers of irony to Sharon and Ozzy pairing up and shaking their mojo that you are tempted to lose sight of the core facts.

In the first place, Sharon wasn't initially interested in Ozzy either as a business proposition or as a lover. When Ozzy's band Black Sabbath first approached Machat and Machat in LA to help them switch to the Ardens in 1979, Sharon could hardly contain her excitement.

But she wasn't interested in Ozzy at first. She had developed a passion for Sabbath guitarist Tony Iommi, but was also out of luck because the rocker wasn't in the least bit interested.

Sharon would later develop a real crush on the man who would replace Ozzy in Black Sabbath: the iron-lunged Ronnie Dio.

There was one small problem: Ronnie's wife, Wendy Gaxiola. She also happened to be his manager. Wendy proved more than a match for Sharon and made sure that she got the message that Ronnie was strictly off limits.

Sharon certainly had her 'passions'. For a while she was fixated on guitarists Gary Moore and Glen Hughes, who was with Deep Purple. They both got their solo Jet contracts in due course thanks to Sharon.

Sharon had actually been 'retired' from the family business by 1981. During the summer of 1981 I went on the road with the Blizzard of Ozz, overseeing the tour in Canada. When I got back to New York, I told my father and Don that a heavy metal rock and roll manager was not what I wanted to be. Don wanted his son David to replace me. Don and his wife Pat had no desire for Sharon to be a manager. But fate was to change everything.

First, her brother David's wife Jane went through a traumatic premature birth that meant they were grounded in London, which meant that Sharon had to go back out on the road. Someone had to watch Ozzy and the band on their tour. Perhaps her father really wanted a way out of the madness, so he threw Sharon back in.

So it was only when no-one wanted to take on Ozzy that Sharon came back into the Jet fold and subsequently turned her hand to managing him. For Don, it was sweet music. At first.

Don was determined to re-invent himself as the manager of some money-spinning Las Vegas act a la Elvis Presley. He believed that his ticket to freedom lay with the band Air Supply, whose bland MOR-style soft rock fitted the Vegas bill perfectly.

He had found that their Australian record label, Big Time Records, run as well as owned by their management team of Fred Bestall and Lance Reynolds, had been taking the band for two commissions and sought to exploit this choice morsel for all it was worth.

The truth was that Don operated exactly the same game with his bands but if the Ardens were aware of rampant hypocrisy, I never saw it.

Don started putting the squeeze on Bestall and Reynolds after approaching the band and telling them that they could do much better elsewhere. That was shorthand for 'Let me manage you and everything will be OK'.

Bestall and Reynolds were terrified and looked around for someone who they thought could offer some protection against the Ardens. They heard the Machats might fit that particular bill.

I was called in to arbitrate between the warring parties, but in truth this was no contest. Bestall and Reynolds were so terrified by Don's reputation that there was little I could do.

When they were in my office for a teleconference with Don, I put the speaker phone on and sat back and listened to Don work his magic. He said: 'Steven, I don't care if they are your clients. You know what I can do to them if I want: their breathing will stop. Tell them to fucking behave.'

The terrified managers turned to me but I could barely focus on them – I was laughing so hard that I had to put the phone on mute.

'What are you laughing at?' they asked.

I said: 'He's full of shit. You always need to reflect on who is in the room with Don when he makes those kind of remarks. It's all bullshit. He wants to create this hardman image. Don't fall for it.'

But they took him at his word. They told everyone that Don threatened to kill them. Air Supply switched to the Ardens after I brokered a peace settlement, which saw everyone make money.

Bestall and Reynolds got a greatest hits album and Clive Davis and his Arista record label got a huge record as he was the man in the middle, the distributing record label during the dispute between Don and the Bestall Reynolds team.

The irony was that the band never really broke Vegas, and nor did Don.

When Don was caught up in the criminal court case involving allegations that he had beaten accountant Harshad Patel, who Don claimed had been defrauding Jet, his luck was beginning to run out. Although Don was subsequently acquitted, he had lost Air Supply and, more importantly, Jet had crashed and burned in his absence.

His career would never recover.

Ozzy first found fame with heavy metal outfit Black Sabbath, which he had helped form in 1968 in his home town of

Birmingham, England.

Sabbath would become one of the top five definitive heavy metal groups of all time with their mix of the occult, deafening rock and harmonic vocals.

Osbourne was the frontman for Sabbath and had a lovely voice, but he was not the creative force behind the band. That honour lay with guitarist Tony Iommi and the lyrics from Geezer Butler. They were managed by the Arden's former associates and later deadly rivals the Meehans, and signed to Warner Records in the US and Phonogram for the rest of the world.

When their publishing contract was up for renewal, the Meehans dispatched their hard man, my friend William Mamone, to get Ozzy's name on the dotted line. Mamone turned up with a lot of blow and agreed to entertain Ozzy up in a house until he re-signed. Ozzy did as he was bid.

But by 1979 the band were getting tired of the Meehans and Warners. They wanted out and approached the Ardens, who initially were only too happy to take up the chance to screw the Meehans.

Tempting as it is to dismiss Ozzy as some role model for the soon-to-be movie *Spinal Tap*, with its portrayal of the stereotypical British rocker whose IQ was only marginally higher than his age, the lead singer of Black Sabbath had a good brain. And he had an extremely melodic voice.

But Ozzy was aware he had issues. When we first met in my office in 2049 Century Park East in the spring of 1979, the conversation did, however, have its Spinal Tap moments. With his thick Birmingham accent, Ozzy sounded like a buzz saw on Mogadon. Crying he said: 'Man, I am the most fucked up creature you will ever meet. Just look at my hands for a start.' Osbourne held up his fists and told me to look at his knuckles. 'I'm so fucked up, I can't even spell my name right.' Sure enough, his first name was spelt Ozie across the four knuckles.

'I've tripped every day of my life. Spent one year on a park bench and every single day dropped acid. I'm bloody paranoid to be honest. I even pee on myself. I don't like managers or lawyers because they can't handle shit like this. Are you really up to handling clients like me?'

I smiled: 'I couldn't think of anything I would enjoy more. In fact, when you have one of your out of body experiences, perhaps you could tell me what you see.'

Ozzy wasn't as dumb as he sometimes pretended to be. He knew he was setting me up for the punchline to see if I was up to the mark. I think he even staged the knuckle name thing, to test me.

We hit it off and developed a rapport that would stay in place until Sharon fucked everything up. Her problem was that I wouldn't side with her, so she began to distance me from Ozzy.

This was ironic really, because I know that I look for the dark side and dark energy. I am drawn to the underdog and I'm drawn to trouble and the people who generate it. Sharon sure fitted that particular bill, but believe me, she's just difficult to be drawn to.

But as I scouted around for a deal for Sabbath, I had to face an uncomfortable reality.

The US was in the grip of the disco craze and no-one was interested in the group, least of all CBS who we thought were the ideal match for Sabbath as they had no metal artists. But they wouldn't touch Sabbath.

Ozzy lost what remained of the plot. He didn't like the idea of any turbulence and moved into a kind of booze and drugs transcendence.

This was the last straw for his bandmates, who had grown tired of Ozzy's trail of wanton destruction and unparalleled excess. Black Sabbath sacked their lead singer, as well as Jet, and were promptly welcomed back into the Warners stable.

This, in turn, signalled the end for the Ardens and Jet. Their relationship with Black Sabbath drew to a close. But Don had taken a shine to Ozzy, took him under his wing and into his home.

Suddenly I was pitching Ozzy to CBS as a solo act. They didn't want to know and Machat and Machat were beginning to lose their air of invincibility, not least because ELO's star was falling. CBS didn't believe the Ardens could have another hit act: one was enough. They told us that we should concentrate on ELO.

This would ensure that Ozzy bore a grudge towards CBS for the beginning of his solo career; however, under our deal CBS had to release *Blizzard of Oz* under our UK deal. Although it didn't rack up huge sales it was a critical success that would mark it as a future sleeper hit within the next six months.

At that point our options were strictly limited, because Warners, which was really the only other heavyweight label with big money to hand, wanted nothing to do with Don. The Ardens had screwed Warners over the ELO contracts and they had neither forgotten nor forgiven my business partner Don.

Mo Ostin at Warners warned me: 'I don't resent the fact that you are representing Don Arden and I hope they are paying you a ton of money, but just be careful – they're not like you or me.'

This infuriated Don and motivated him to set up the band Blizzard of Ozz, with Ozzy as the lead singer, because he wanted to prove his critics wrong. They promptly recorded two complete albums from Blizzard, with Don and David Arden acting as executive producers, despite the fact that no US label was interested. But when I was on the verge of selling the Blizzard albums to Rupert Perry at Capitol, CBS got whiff of a deal.

We were called into Walter Yetnikoff's office and given a verbal beating. 'I find it humiliating that you are selling my act to another label. If you proceed with this deal, we will close down Jet and ELO.'

The claim that Blizzard was a CBS act was ridiculous. They had rejected Ozzy from the off, but when I pointed that out, Walter rejected this out of hand.

My father and Don Arden folded real quick but managed to

impose one condition: Ozzy would not be cross collateralised against Jet's losses. The albums came out a year early in the UK because, as I just stated above, under the terms of the Jet deal CBS UK had to press and manufacture any albums we supplied.

To protect all interests, I opened up a company in Nevada called Princess Productions, which covered our end of the deal. This was me and Sharon taking care of our fathers. I incorporated the company, taking the roles of vice-president and treasurer, and Sharon was secretary and president.

But the 15 per cent cut I was promised hasn't been seen to this day.

Three years after the first Jet US deal at CBS, it was Myron Roth in the same office. This time, Ozzy was going to get a solo deal and came along for the ride, even if he had to be dragged along kicking and screaming. Ozzy was upset that he was part of CBS because they had already rejected him once. He was pissed off with me for lining up the deal and wanted to sink it by grossing CBS out.

He brought in this dead canary in his pocket, took it out, bit off its head and spat it out into the lap of this CBS PR woman. Roth was outraged and tried to throw Ozzy off the label, but then the records started selling. The greenback imperative kicked in again and Yetnikoff told Roth it wasn't his call: money first and principle second.

The letter that Myron had sent to me telling me that Ozzy was due to be dropped was, of course, never publicised. Instead they sent out the picture of the lady from CBS, with her face covered, with this dead bird in her lap and captioned it 'Lunch with Ozzy', as if this was one big hoot. Money talks and bullshit walks.

Ozzy's solo career would grow and then flatten, but few heavy metal fans would deny its high point was Blizzard. *Blizzard of Oz* came out in 1980 in the UK and 1981 in the US, where it would eventually sell more than four million copies.

Although it would later be billed as Ozzy's first two solo albums, the real creative power behind the throne lay with a trio of session musicians: guitarist Randy Rhoads, Rainbow bassist Bob Daisley, and drummer Lee Kerslake, who was with rock group Uriah Heep. I made sure CBS signed Ozzy on a solo deal because I didn't want to waste my time negotiating with the lawyers representing the other members of Blizzard. The irony was that CBS made this easy for me because they didn't realise where the creative drive lay.

Rhoads would be dead within a year of the album's release Stateside. He was in a light plane in March 1982 with two others when they apparently thought it would be funny to buzz the tour bus with Ozzy and Sharon sleeping inside it. They managed the first two times but the third fly past saw their luck run out. The plane's wing clipped the bus and crashed into a nearby southern mansion, which was owned by Jerry Calhoun who had leased us the tour bus.

Nevertheless Blizzard produced two albums that were to prove the high point of Ozzy's 'solo' career. It would be downhill ever after. Sharon wasn't happy that Kerslake, Rhoads and Daisley had such a large creative input into Ozzy's music. More accurately, she wasn't happy for them to share the credit. I found this kind of funny, because the truth was that Ozzy was barely capable of making the studio recording sessions, he was in such a bad state. At the time it was too much drugs and booze for Ozzy. He depended on his bandmates for much of the creative input.

But when Sharon took control of Ozzy's career, she seemed to take against anyone who threatened Ozzy's image of creative genius or, more to the point, threatened her meal ticket. Kerslake and Daisley also told me that Sharon constantly, whether in jest or in reality, demanded that they individually fulfil her sexual appetite. She was one of the few women, if any, that could successfully manage a heavy rock act in the rock and roll era.

She assumed the role of rock and roll manager, regardless of the fact she wasn't a male.

Sure enough, both Kerslake and Daisley were fired in the summer of 1981 and their names were erased from the album credits as if they had never even existed. Ozzy's career would never again touch the heights of Blizzard of Ozz, despite his best efforts to drum up publicity.

In February 1982, I had a dinner with the then First Lady Nancy Reagan's press secretary Morgan Mason, the son of actor James Mason. Within a week, the significance of this meal became clear when I had a call from Don Arden.

There was a big problem: Ozzy had peed on the Alamo, which was just about as close as America gets to an historical war monument. Ozzy had been on a Blizzard tour that had flunked ticket sales in San Antonio, Texas, and, thoroughly disillusioned, had donned a dress and wandered off around the nearby Alamo.

Stoned and drunk, he had been desperate for a toilet and when none was forthcoming, Ozzy decided to raise his dress and relieve himself. He had been arrested and was in serious trouble. Nowadays, Ozzy would have been given a full body cavity search by the Department of Homeland Security and shipped off to Guantanamo Bay.

All the same, he was in imminent danger of being kicked out of the US and that would have spelt the end of his career. This was no laughing matter and we needed to find a solution quickly.

I called Morgan and got a meeting. At the meeting, he looked at me and said: 'I think I know the answer. Ozzy needs to make a generous donation to Nancy Reagan's drug programme: Keep America Drug Free. I'll speak to Nancy and set the whole thing up.'

Sure enough, Don shipped the money to Mrs Reagan and the potential Ozzy charges disappeared and the immigration problems went with them. Don told me that he had paid out '$100,000 for that cunt' Ozzy.

The funny thing was that I saw Ozzy in the Jet offices the day after the Alamo drama and asked him what on earth this incident was all about. Ozzy said: 'I couldn't handle the fucking irony of all the Americans fighting for freedom from the Mexicans and then all you see guarding this shrine are fucking Mexicans.'

I couldn't help but laugh and told him that the Americans had fought as mercenaries simply to get the Texans free of the Mexican yoke. Twelve years later the US would eventually end up with a country from east coast to west coast. The war started because cotton barons in north Mexico refused to accept the ban on slavery imposed by the Mexican government in 1829.

Ozzy was not impressed with my history lesson. 'You're a cunt, Steven. The only reason I pissed on the Alamo was because this was the first show on our tour that hadn't sold enough tickets.'

In 1986 both Kerslake and Daisley successfully sued Jet and had their songwriting and performance credits reinstated. But the group name had been changed to Ozzy Osbourne so their lawyers were no great shakes.

They both argued that Blizzard of Ozz was a band, not simply a solo project that cast them in the roles of sidemen. But contracts were never signed because, according to them, Jet kept stalling. In the end they got their money for the sales up to that date, but for all subsequent sales they would never receive another cent. Once Sharon had got control of the masters she decided that the band members were side musicians and not entitled to any future artist royalties. In the process, Sharon ignited a feud with Daisley and Kerslake that would stretch for nearly another two decades, as we shall see. It would also see Sharon pitted against her father, again.

I was sitting in my home, late one Saturday evening in October 1999, and from the moment I lifted the receiver, I knew it was Sharon on the other end of the line, even though we hadn't spoken for years. It was just I could hear the screaming long before the receiver reached my ear.

Her charge, as far as I could make sense of what she was saying, was that I was trying to sell Ozzy Osbourne material to Suge Knight at Death Row records. Considering that Death Row was the home of gangsta rap, the idea was a little far fetched, but that didn't stop Sharon.

'Steven? Is that you, you cunt? You worthless piece of shit. What the fuck do you think you are up to? You've no right to sell Ozzy to Death Row and if you do I'll fucking come after you. Do you fucking understand me?'

I knew I should rise above the abuse but instead I couldn't resist baiting Sharon. 'Sharon: lovely to hear from you. Long time no speak.'

She cut me dead. 'Don't give me that shit. You always were a cunt and always will be.'

I couldn't resist it. 'This from a woman who couldn't even use a knife or fork when I first met her,' I replied. Sharon used to eat with her fingers to gross out her Dad's guests. I was on a roll: 'Sharon, you need to get your facts right first when you start talking about family. You need to think about your own family, not mine. Your mother is dying and it's time you started speaking to her again. See your parents again, Sharon. You shouldn't keep on treating them this way. No Mom, no Dad: no Sharon.'

With that that piece of advice Sharon slammed the phone down and we were done. At least for the time being. Just a month before, I'd had an altogether more pleasant surprise at the other end of the line: her father.

We hadn't spoken for a few years but we immediately clicked into gear. It really felt like we had slipped back to 1978. Ever to the point, Don said: 'I need to see you right now.'

We met at Nate 'n' Al's Deli in Beverly Hills. Don had a business proposition: he had tapes, records and videos from most of his famous groups and asked me to help him sell them in return for a slice of the action. He told me he owned the copyright to them, and that was good enough for me. He would later sign those Ozzie masters over to me to continue to exploit.

I told him that I had been approached by a friend with connections to this internet company called Musicmaker who were looking for material to sell online.

It fast became clear that Don's most marketable property was a taped video concert of the Blizzard of Ozz featuring Ozzy. I promised him that I would sound Musicmaker out and get back to him. We then set business aside. Don started confessing to me and crying about his life and his family's relationships.

Don said: 'Ozzy ran away from Sharon, you know? He called me up asking me to come to the Beverly Hills Hotel. He wanted me to protect him from her. Ozzy called me because he had realised he had no control over his life.'

Don's anger at Sharon, who had not spoken to him courteously for over a decade, was constantly bubbling over during our ensuing conversation.

He said: 'She's a cunt. She's told my own grandchildren that I'm dead. I don't know what to do. She will not even see her own mother, let alone talk to her.' We were both in tears at this point. I told him that my daughter Margaux was hanging with Sharon's daughter Kelly, and Margaux had told me that Kelly thought her grandfather was dead.

I swore to Don that I would do my best to get him a deal because I believed that one way or another this was my chance to bring issues to a head between Don and Sharon and satisfy my karma. I knew she would go insane to hear that we were reunited. We parted, promising to keep in contact.

After the inevitable horsetrading, Musicmaker eventually paid out $100,000 for the tape with my commission agreed at 20 per cent. Even there, though, half of my fee went to the man who introduced me to Musicmaker. He had to split his $10,000 with the bosses at Musicmaker! Everyone was getting a slice of the pie. The video is what Don gave me for the future.

The irony was that Sharon had only picked up on the rumours, not the facts. My friend David Mishery at Death Row put out the false whisper that I was selling Ozzy material to Suge's label. He thought that the idea was kinda funny. He had a point.

When Sharon had called Mishery to dress him down, David said, 'Why not call Steven and tell him what you think.' His idea of a joke was to give Sharon my home number.

Nine months later, I got a call from a Beverly Hills lawyer called Tom Brackley. I'd just seen a $250,000 fee regarding comic man Stan Lee go south that very day, so I was not in a good mood and chewed him up. But Brackley persisted and told me that his firm needed my help because it was representing Bob Daisley and Lee Kerslake in a legal action against Sharon and Ozzy Osbourne. I was stunned because I thought the case had died in 1986.

In actual fact the dispute had flared up again in 1997. Bass guitarist Daisley and Kerslake, who played drums, had sued over a compilation album released under Ozzy's name a few years earlier called *Ozzman Cometh*, which relied on material from The Blizzard of Ozz.

This included several songs that Daisley had written and performed but on the liner notes he was called 'Bob Daisy.' This would prove the last straw. But with their action apparently going nowhere, Daisley had recommended me to their lawyers because he knew I knew the full story behind the rise, fall and rise again of Ozzy and Sharon Osbourne.

After meeting Brackley at the Beverly Hills Hotel we cut a deal. I became a consultant to their action against the Osbournes in return for 25 per cent of their third of the settlement and with the legal firm helping me out professionally with my bands.

The first thing I did for their attorneys was set up a series of meetings with Don Arden in 2000. Don agreed to do the right thing by the boys and tell in his testimony the whole unvarnished truth: Daisley and Kerslake had been royally screwed. Affidavits were drawn up which said that Blizzard was a group recording with Ozzy as the vocalist and the group should split the royalties. Daisley and Kerslake were not sidemen or session musicians playing for a fee. They were equal members of the group and co-owners of the proceeds.

We all met up for a few drinks to see if we could reach an agreement, which we could, and also took the chance to swap tales of Sharon.

Don was blunt when he discussed his motives. 'I want to destroy the cunt. Do you know what Sharon said to me when I told her that her mother was dying and Sharon should talk to her again? She turned around to me and said "Let me know when she's dead so that I can come over and pee on the grave".'

The truth is that Don wanted to see his grandchildren and knew that he had to try and bridge the divide with Sharon somehow. Don also knew that his daughter was probably the one person in the world who was most like him. I think that fact alone gave them this love/hate relationship.

When Brackley's partner John Freund visited Don in London in August 2001, he was handed a treasure trove of material. Unfortunately for me, Don's son David was present at one of the meetings between Don and Freund, and began to realise what was going on. When he found out I was involved, David started pressing the alarm buttons. When Don wouldn't listen to him and drop his involvement in the case, David went to Sharon.

Suddenly, Sharon wanted a rapprochement with the father she had called 'dead', which was very touching and very convenient. Sharon was worried I could upset her bread basket, and she played her best card: she told Don he could see his grandchildren before he died.

Sharon's strategy not only brought Don back into the fold, it also screwed our action against her and Ozzy. If she and Ozzy had lost, they would have had to pay up to 75 per cent of Blizzard's current and past earnings to Daisley and Kerslake and the Rhoads estate, and that would have amounted to millions that they simply didn't have. This was right before the MTV show that made her a celebrity.

When I read that Sharon claimed that the carnage unleashed by 9/11 had spurred on the family to heal old wounds, I had to admire her nerve. Coming only a month after her father had coughed his guts to our lawyers, this seemed like an incredible coincidence.

But I had no bad blood. I could understand Don's logic in giving way to Sharon over the Blizzard action. In reality, all Don wanted was a rapprochement with his daughter. Don was beginning to suffer from Alzheimer's and he knew his days were numbered. So did I. I was asked by people on my side to pursue Don for perjury, but I refused. I didn't hate Sharon, for all her hatred and our history. From the start, I'd wanted to do the right thing by Don and if that meant walking away from the action, then so be it. Don did give me at the time a tape of his where he tells all his Sharon stories, for me to hold in case we ever needed it. He asked me one day, please tell the truth about her and I.

In 2002 the inevitable happened and the Daisley and Kerslake action came to a grinding halt. The suit had nowhere to go and because Don had withdrawn his evidence and testimony, their case was never tested in court. The same year, the albums were re-issued again and this time Daisley and Kerslake's original drum and bass tracks were erased and replaced. Sharon had her revenge after what was portrayed as a convincing victory over their detractors. She made her own history.

I met Don one more time, in a one-bedroom LA apartment. It was sad, because this was a man who had once owned one of the largest houses in Hollywood and now, here he was, in some small apartment in the outskirts of Beverly Hills. It seemed a bitter case of how far he had fallen.

When we embraced we both cried. He said: 'You understand what I did?'

I said: 'Yes, I fully understand.'

He said: 'It's only money.'

I replied: 'More importantly, you get to see your family.'

Don said: 'That's what I love about you. You understand. Stay being yourself and you will be last man standing.'

Don told me that the deal was straightforward: Sharon bought him off and gave him access to the grandchildren, in return for sinking the action against Sharon and her meal ticket.

His family kept Don well away from me during his final years, which I bitterly regret. I knew that they were moving him around from the grapevine, but when his telephone number changed I got the message.

I was not even invited to his funeral in 2007 and didn't even know about it until it was in the newspapers.

But even in his death, Sharon had to have the last say. She refused to have him buried alongside his wife and Sharon's mother, Hope.

Schillings
Lawyers

Farrer & Co
66 Lincoln's Inn Fields
London
WC2A 3 LH

By facsimile and email: 020 7405 2296/jcp@farrer.co.uk

Our Ref: JK/JO/an/O0042/008
Your ref: JCP/MXP/66155/1

16 July 2009

Dear Sirs

SHARON AND OZZY OSBOURNE

We refer to your letter dated 13 July 2009.

We note that your client claims that it is satisfied of the evidence it has concerning the matters complained of. We have made our position clear as to the paucity of such evidence and your client proceeds to publish the allegations complained of at its peril.

However, the evidence described in your letter dated 13 July 2009 that is relied upon by your client is unreliable. We enclose with this letter copies of witness statements from Bob Daisley and Lee Kerslake. Those statements confirm beyond doubt that the allegation made by Mr Machat in respect of Messrs Daisley and Kerslake is untrue.

We are instructed that whilst Messrs Daisley and Kerslake may have met Mr Machat briefly in New York in September 2001 there was no conversation of the type alleged by Mr Machat.

We understand that Mr Machat was accompanied at such meeting by Thomas Brackey. Please confirm that this is the same Thomas Brackey who worked as a lawyer with Mr Machat in the law firm Freund & Brackey LLP and was a co-defendant together with Mr Machat in the case of *Delmar Arnaud v Steven Elliot Machat*.

SCHILLINGS 41 Bedford Square, London WC1B 3HX
Tel 020 7034 9000 · Fax 020 7034 9200
Email legal@schillings.co.uk · Online www.schillings.co.uk · DX Number 89265 (Soho Square 1)

Regulated by the Solicitors Regulation Authority
Partners: Rachel Atkins · Gideon Benaim · Rod Christie-Miller · John Kelly · Keith Schilling · Simon Smith

Given that we do not see what other source other than Mr Brackey could be relied upon by your client to support this contention, we reserve the right to refer to this ruling, to rebut your bare assertion that Mr Machat's statement has been corroborated by a "reliable third party". If it is the same Mr Brackey, then he is not to be considered a reliable independent source, just as many other of Mr Machat's other sources are demonstrably unreliable and/or vexatious.

Since October of last year, we have supplied numerous and non-exhaustive instances of Mr Machat (and thereby your client) placing reliance on unreliable sources, of telling untruths and concocting defamatory fantasies concerning our clients.

Many of these questions have been ignored by you and your client (insofar as no response, whether of a satisfactory nature or alternatively, at all) have been provided to us. The fact that much of the original text has been discarded or subject to alteration does of course tell its own story as to the veracity of the Book and your and your client's faith in Mr Machat.

Throughout our correspondence we have demonstrated that the decision by your client to proceed with publishing any of the allegations would be grossly irresponsible, reckless and malicious. We have advised our clients that publication of the Book by your client in the current form will lead to an irresistible claim for aggravated and exemplary damages by our clients against your client and its directors.

We also note that Beautiful Book's website states that the Book has been selected as Mojo magazine's 'Book of the Month' for August. We understand that the August edition of Mojo is due in newsagents this week. Please confirm by return:

1. Which other third parties were provided with a copy of the Book?

2. Please confirm which version(s) of the Book were supplied to those third parties.

3. In the event that any version of the Book has been sent to those third parties please provide a copy by return.

When responding, please also confirm whether you are instructed by Mr Machat, a question you stated you were taking instructions on in your letter dated 6 July 2009.

We continue to reserve all of our clients' rights.

Yours faithfully

Schillings

SCHILLINGS

WITNESS STATEMENT OF BOB DAISLEY

I, Bob Daisley will say as follows:

1. I am a musician and songwriter and have been a member of several different bands throughout my career.

2. I make this statement in support of Sharon Osbourne's complaint about an allegation contained in what I understand to be a copy of a manuscript of a book which is to be published in the UK in August of this year entitled "Gods, Gangsters and Honour" by Steven Machat ("the Book").

3. I have been informed by Messrs Schillings, acting on behalf of Sharon and Ozzy Osbourne that the Book contains an allegation that Lee Kerslake and I had told Mr Machat that while we were working with Ozzy Osbourne, Sharon Osbourne had constantly, whether in jest or in reality, demanded that we fulfil her sexual appetite. The relevant extract from the Book is as follows:

   "Kerslake and Daisley also told me [i.e. Mr Machat] that Sharon constantly, whether in jest or in reality, demanded that they individually fulfil her sexual appetite"

4. The claim attributed to me is not true.

5. To the best of my recollection I have only had a small number of conversations with Mr Machat in or around 2000/2001 in connection with a court case.

293502.1

6. I am happy to confirm for the record that the allegation is completely false. The supposed incidents concerning me described in the Book did not take place. Sharon Osbourne never once tried to coerce or otherwise harass me into having sex with her, even as a joke.

STATEMENT OF TRUTH

I believe that the facts stated in this witness statement are true.

Signed...

BOB DAISLEY

Dated: 15 July 2009

293502_1

WITNESS STATEMENT OF LEE KERSLAKE

I, Lee Kerslake will say as follows:

1. I am a musician and songwriter and have been a member of several different bands throughout my career.

2. I make this statement in support of Sharon Osbourne's complaint about an allegation contained in what I understand to be a copy of a manuscript of a book which is to be published in the UK in August of this year entitled *"Gods, Gangsters and Honour"* by Steven Machat ("the Book").

3. I have been informed by Messrs Schillings, acting on behalf of Sharon and Ozzy Osbourne that the Book contains an allegation that Bob Daisley and I had told Mr Machat that while we were working with Ozzy Osbourne, Sharon Osbourne had constantly, whether in jest or in reality, demanded that we fulfil her sexual appetite. The relevant extract from the Book is as follows:

   "Kerslake and Daisley also told me [i.e. Mr Machat] that Sharon constantly, whether in jest or in reality, demanded that they individually fulfil her sexual appetite"

4. The claim attributed to me is not true.

5. I am happy to confirm for the record that the allegation is completely false. The supposed incidents concerning me described in the Book

did not take place. Sharon Osbourne never once tried to coerce or otherwise harass me into having sex with her, even as a joke.

STATEMENT OF TRUTH

I believe that the facts stated in this witness statement are true.

Signed..

LEE KERSLAKE

Dated: 15 July 2009

FARRER&Co

Schillings
Solicitors
DX 89265 (Soho Square 1)

Your reference	JK/JO/an/00042/008
Our reference	JCP/MXP/nl
Direct telephone	020 7917 7217
Direct facsimile	020 7405 2296
Direct email	jcp@farrer.co.uk

13 July 2009

By Fax: 020 7034 9200
By Post

Dear Sirs

Your clients: Sharon and Ozzy Osbourne
Our client: Beautiful Books Limited

We refer to your letter of Friday.

Whilst we note what you say, our client is satisfied about the evidence it has of the matters complained of. This includes the fact of Steven Machat having met both Bob Daisley and Lee Kerslake. Indeed, this has been corroborated by a reliable third party who has confirmed that Mr Machat was with Messrs Daisley and Kerslake in New York on 11 September 2001.

As regards your request for an undertaking in respect of "defamatory allegations", at the risk of repeating ourselves, we do not accept that all those matters you have raised are capable of bearing a defamatory meaning and, to the extent they may be found to be defamatory, which is not admitted, our client is satisfied it will be able to justify the claims made.

In respect of the second undertaking you demand, as we have previously advised you, the print date for the book was last Friday and, accordingly, the book is now in the process of being printed. Had you wished to have made an application for an injunction the proper time to have done so was prior to last Friday. Your clients have had plenty of time to apply but have seemingly chosen not to do so.

If your clients now wish to proceed to apply for an injunction, presumably they have been advised on the need for a cross-undertaking in damages.

Yours faithfully

arrer & Co LLP 66 Lincoln's Inn Fields London WC2A 3LH **Telephone** +44 (0)20 7242 2022 **Facsimile** +44 (0)20 7242 9899

X 32 Chancery Lane **Website** www.farrer.co.uk

arrer & Co LLP is a limited liability partnership registered in England and Wales, registered number OC323670, and is regulated by the Solicitors Regulation Authority. FARDM1-1338590.1

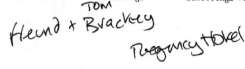

PRIVATE AND CONFIDENTIAL
Farrer & Co
66 Linolns Inn Fields
London
WC2A 3 LH

By facsimile and email: 020 7405 2296
jcp@farrer.co.uk

Our Ref: JK/JO/an/O0042/008
Your ref: JCP/MXP/68155/1

10 July 2009

Dear Sirs

SHARON AND OZZY OSBOURNE

We refer to previous correspondence and in particular paragraph 3 of your letter
dated 6 July 2009.

You state *"we are instructed Daisley and Kerslake will, if required, confirm this
information"*.

Your clients' claim is untrue.

We have spoken with Bob Daisley and Lee Kerslake. In summary:

1. Both Bob Daisley and Lee Kerslake have confirmed that the claims
   attributed to them in the Book are untrue and that they have not spoken
   to Mr Machat about the Book or such allegations.

2. Both Bob Daisley and Lee Kerslake have confirmed that Sharon
   Osbourne <u>never</u>, whether in jest or in seriousness, demanded sexual
   behaviour from either of them.

3. Lee Kerslake has, to the best of his knowledge, never met or spoken to
   Steven Machat.

SCHILLINGS 41 Bedford Square, London WC1B 3HX
Tel 020 7034 9000 · Fax 020 7034 9200
Email legal@schillings.co.uk · Online www.schillings.co.uk · DX Number 89265 (Soho Square 1)

Regulated by the Solicitors Regulation Authority
Partners: Rachel Atkins · Gideon Benaim · Rod Christie-Miller · John Kelly · Keith Schilling · Simon Smith

25 YEA
Protecting rights and

293248_2

Schillings
Lawyers

4. Bob Daisley had a number of short conversations with Steven Machat around the time of the lawsuit in 2000. He has not spoken to Mr Machat about the allegations as Mr Machat claims.

The above demonstrates that not only are Mr Machat's claims fantasy, but so is the assertion that witnesses are prepared to support his fantasies. Mr Machat has simply had no contact with these people. How then, as claimed in your letter, can your clients say that Mr Machat's claims will be *"confirmed as true"*? Your clients are either being seriously misled, or of more concern are proceeding to publish allegations that it knows are defamatory and untenable. Your clients must not publish the allegations complained of.

In addition to the other defamatory allegations which you are already on notice of, we have repeatedly informed you, that this specific allegation is grossly defamatory. The two witnesses who you rely on in your letter of 6 July 2009 have confirmed to us that what you say in your letter is false. Your clients cannot now maintain their position with regard to *Sunderland Housing* i.e. your clients cannot now say that they intend to justify this allegation as being true in circumstances where the three principals have confirmed that the claim is not true.

As you are now aware from our second letter of yesterday these are not the only individuals in this position, with David Arden, Richard Chemel, Michael Magliari, Kelly Osbourne, Ozzy Osbourne and Sharon Osbourne all confirming that Mr Machat's claims are fantasy.

We have also previously informed you that any decision by your clients to proceed with publishing any of the allegations would be grossly irresponsible, reckless and malicious. We require you to provide your undertaking on behalf of your clients that:

1. The defamatory allegations complained of will not be published by your clients or any third party on their behalf, and

2. To the extent that any Books have been printed that make such defamatory allegations they will be destroyed and a certificate of destruction evidenced by a statement of truth provided.

Should you refuse to do so your clients' untenable conduct will be drawn to the attention of the court.

In our second letter of yesterday we asked that you respond to us on two points by return. We require a proper response to be provided as well as the undertakings sought by no later than **2pm on Monday 13 July 2009**.

In the event that your clients fail to provide such undertaking we will advise our clients to seek injunctive relief to prevent publication of the Book. Any printing costs that your clients incur, given that it is on notice of our clients' claims are accordingly incurred at your clients' own risk, as we will require any copies of the Book containing the allegations to be held securely pursuant to court order and destroyed upon the successful conclusion of litigation in our clients' favour.

We also require confirmation as to whether you are also instructed by Mr Machat in relation to this matter.

In the circumstances legal proceedings will include claims for aggravated and exemplary damages and costs (which are rising significantly) on an indemnity basis against Beautiful Books, its Directors, Managing Director and Mr Machat. These shall be in addition to the usual damages for libel (including special damages) to which our clients remain of course entitled.

We await your reply as a matter of urgency.

All of our clients' rights are reserved.

Yours faithfully

SCHILLINGS

FARRER&Co

Schillings
Solicitors
DX 89265 (Soho Square 1)

Your reference	JK/JO/an/00042/008
Our reference	JCP/MXP/vs
Direct telephone	020 7917 7217
Direct facsimile	020 7405 2296
Direct email	jcp@farrer.co.uk

9 July 2009

By Fax: 020 7034 9200
By Post

Dear Sirs

Your clients: Sharon and Ozzy Osbourne
Our client: Beautiful Books Limited

We are in receipt of your letter sent at 9.17am this morning. We note that despite the fact we sent you our letter of 6 July 2009 three days ago, you have demanded a response by 2.30pm today. Your repeated attempts to set arbitrary deadlines in this matter are unreasonable.

We have provided you with the two chapters of the book that refer to your clients and in this regard we have also already set out our client's position in relation to the points you raise. In the circumstances, we see little benefit in repeating ourselves and accordingly we do not intend to answer the questions you raise at this stage, although we will of course do this should it be necessary (in the event your clients decide to proceed with their threat to seek an injunction against our client). As we have advised you, both we and our client are quite aware of our client's obligations in relation to *Sunderland Housing* and our client will meet those obligations if called upon. There is no requirement for it to deal with this matter at this stage.

We have previously informed you that the print date of the book is today. For the avoidance of doubt, our client still intends to proceed with printing the book today.

We fully reserve all of our client's rights, including the right to deal with such points as raised in your letter as may be necessary to address in due course.

Yours faithfully

[signature]

rer & Co LLP 66 Lincoln's Inn Fields London WC2A 3LH Telephone +44 (0)20 7242 2022 Facsimile +44 (0)20 7242 9899
32 Chancery Lane Website www.farrer.co.uk

er & Co LLP is a limited liability partnership registered in England and Wales, registered number OC323570, and is regulated by the Solicitors Regulation Authority, FARDM1-1336701.1
of the members of the LLP is displayed at the above address, together with a list of those non-members who are designated as partners

Schillings
Lawyers

PRIVATE AND CONFIDENTIAL
Farrer & Co
66 Lincoln's Inn Fields
London
WC2A 3 LH

By facsimile and email: 020 7405 2296/jcp@farrer.co.uk

Our Ref: JK/JO/an/O0042/008
Your ref: JCP/MXP/66155/1
9 July 2009

Dear Sirs

SHARON AND OZZY OSBOURNE

We refer to your letter dated 6 July 2009.

The further amendments that you propose are noted. We further note that you will respond to us on the question of whether you are instructed by Mr Machat. Please confirm the position by return.

Our clients are very concerned that to date there has been little or no realisation on your part and that of your clients that the claims made by Mr Machat are inaccurate, misleading and/or pure fantasy. The amendments which have been to the Book do not address this concern.

Throughout the parts of the Book which we have had sight of, Mr Machat seeks to paint a picture of intimacy with regard to his (supposed) relationship with our clients. He clearly sees himself as being part of the inner sanctum of our clients' business and social circles and that accordingly he may speak about our clients with authority. In fact, Mr Machat was not closely linked to our clients at all. He was not part of their social circle. He worked with Don Arden predominantly in the 1970s and/or early 1980s, not with either of our clients and does not have any insight into our clients.

Whilst we have previously set out at length (albeit on a non exhaustive basis) some of the inaccuracies in the chapters, it is concerning that judging by your letter of 6 July 2009 Mr Machat stands by some of the errors which are demonstrably untrue, namely:

SCHILLINGS 41 Bedford Square, London WC1B 3HX
Tel 020 7034 9000 · Fax 020 7034 9200
Email legal@schillings.co.uk · Online www.schillings.co.uk · DX Number 89265 (Soho Square 1)

Regulated by the Solicitors Regulation Authority
Partners: Rachel Atkins · Gideon Benaim · Rod Christie-Miller · John Kelly · Keith Schilling · Simon Smith

292249_3

Schillings

Lawyers

(i) Ozzy Osbourne did not bite the head of a dead canary. He bit the head of a white dove. Despite his claim in your letter dated 6 July 2009, Mr Machat was not present at the meeting in question. Both of our clients have confirmed this to us. In addition, our clients can obtain confirmation of the fact that Mr Machat was not present from a number of other sources who were, unlike Mr Machat, present at the meeting.

(ii) Kelly Osbourne does not know Margaux Machat. Please confirm whether this is the same Margaux Machat who has spent 11 months in jail and is on probation for 5 years. We refer you to http://recoveringaddictandspoiledbrat.blogspot.com/2008/09/pain-and-probation.html in this regard.

(iii) The suggestion that Ozzy Osbourne misspelled his name on his knuckles, whether staged or otherwise, is pure fantasy.

(iv) The suggestion that Mr Machat was "overseeing" Ozzy Osbourne's tour in Canada is fantasy and is in any event ludicrous. Why would Mr Machat, a lawyer, oversee a rock tour?

Our clients remain in contact with many of the key personnel from that tour, all of whom will be able to confirm that Mr Machat was neither present on the tour nor "overseeing" it. Though you question our clients' ability to accurately remember events from the 1970s and 1980s, we have very specific instructions about Mr Machat and that particular tour. We are instructed that Mr Machat was trying to obtain Ozzy Osbourne's signature on a publishing contract for the benefit of Don Arden. Mr Machat turned up on 2 dates of the tour (in New York and in Canada) to try to meet Ozzy Osbourne. Neither Sharon or Ozzy Osbourne would meet Mr Machat. This may explain why Mr Machat feels he can tell your firm that he was "on the tour". It does not permit him to simply invent material concerning his involvement. His supposed involvement is a fiction.

The point is important because it may help to demonstrate to your client the extent to which the material in the Book is invented and/or inaccurate, often straying in the defamatory and which cannot be justified either morally or legally by either Mr Machat or your client.

There are a number of points in your letter which require further comment from us at this stage. For the avoidance of doubt, the fact that we do not comment

SCHILLINGS 41 Bedford Square, London WC1B 3HX
Tel 020 7034 9000 · Fax 020 7034 9200
Email legal@schillings.co.uk · Online www.schillings.co.uk · DX Number 89265 (Soho Square 1)

Regulated by the Solicitors Regulation Authority
Partners: Rachel Atkins · Gideon Benaim · Rod Christie-Miller · John Kelly · Keith Schilling · Simon Smith

on a particular part of your letter does not mean that we accept what is said. Retaining your numbering:

3. The section in question is considerably more than a comment on Sharon Osbourne's management of the band. The suggestion is that Sharon Osbourne (possibly whilst in a relationship with her then future husband) abused her managerial position to coerce, or otherwise harass, members of Ozzy Osbourne's band into having sex with her. The statement that this may have been "in jest" does nothing to dispel the defamatory insinuation that such approaches for sex may equally well have been made "in reality"; i.e., seriously.

   Further, Messrs Daisley and Kerslake have for more than 25 years held, or given the impression of holding, a grudge against our clients. There have been various lawsuits started by those gentlemen against our clients and/or our clients' businesses. Having embarked on this crusade against our clients many years ago they cannot now be relied upon as unbiased sources in this case. By his own admission Mr Machat does not say that he has heard this information first hand, relying instead upon the (unsworn) word of these disgruntled session musicians.

   It is also important – for the purposes of once again emphasising the lack of truth in the Book - that the allegation concerning Sharon Osbourne's supposed (and denied) "fixation" with Gary Moore and Glen Hughes is addressed. Firstly, it is a fact that Glen Hughes never signed to Jet Records. Whilst Gary Moore did sign to Jet, the entire negotiation on behalf of Jet was carried out by Don and/or David Arden. Sharon Osbourne was not involved in that negotiation at all and had no influence over whether Mr Moore gained a contract or not.

4. It is incorrect for you state that no allegation is made to the effect that Sharon Osbourne acted improperly in the proceedings involving Messrs Daisley and Kerslake. By suggesting that the rapprochement with Don Arden was incredibly "convenient" for our clients, and motivated by a desire to conclude the litigation, the reader is clearly invited to draw the conclusion that Sharon Osbourne put improper pressure on her father to withdraw his evidence from the case. In any event, it is telling that you do not say (as you do in respect of certain other passages containing defamatory allegations) whether your client would attempt to justify this allegation at trial. Would it intend to so? If so, on what evidential basis?

7. We note what you say, although we disagree on the question of whether the allegation is defamatory. The allegation that our client willingly

agreed to make an improper payment (of whatever kind) in order to secure political interference with the legal process that would have resulted in his deportation is plainly capable of causing damage to our client's reputation. There is a distinction between the previously well-documented history of our client's unorthodox behaviour and the suggestion in the Book that his conduct had a sufficiently criminal or unlawful flavour such as to put him at real risk of legal proceedings to secure his deportation from the United States. Despite your general assertion that your client will give an undertaking to justify the allegations in the Book, how can it possibly justify any allegation of this kind? Again, please provide details in accordance with _Sunderland Housing_ (to which we have previously referred in correspondence) as to how your client would propose to make good this charge. Should you fail to do so, the only inference to be drawn will be that your client has no evidence to stand up this allegation.

8. The suggestion that our client would misuse company funds (which is implicit in the references to Sharon Osbourne "spending Jet's money" and Mr Machat "blocking" the alleged purchase of the Mercedes – an action he would not have been able to take, were the story true, if the money belonged to Sharon Osbourne personally) in order to ingratiate herself with Mr Mamone in return for future favours (whether sexual or otherwise) is plainly defamatory. Mr Machat was not the company accountant. Even had he wanted to, he would have been unable to "block" the transaction as claimed. We remind you that Mr Mamone is a convicted felon who has already boasted to Sharon Osbourne that "Steven Machat is my friend. You know who I am with my friends. I lie, steal and cheat for my friends". Mr Mamone is not a reliable source. For Mr Machat to rely on him as a source despite the above will sound in aggravated and/or exemplary damages. You baldly state that "if required, this allegation will be defended as true", yet you notably fail to elaborate upon the basis of such a defence. Once again, and in accordance with _Sunderland Housing_ please outline the evidential basis on which your client would seek to defend this allegation as "true". At present, your failure to do so invites the adverse inference that your client simply has no evidence capable of justifying this charge.

The comments made in your point 11 also require further examination. You say that Mr Simon Petherick, a director of your client, has listened to the supposed tape recording of Don Arden and is satisfied that Don Arden is of sound mind. If that is the case, please confirm:

(a) How did Mr Petherick know that the voice he was hearing was that of Don Arden?

(b) What experience or expertise does Mr Petherick have to call upon to judge whether someone is of sound mind or otherwise?

(c) What was the purpose of the recording?

(d) When was the recording made?

When responding to the above please confirm whether our clients feature in any other part of the Book. In the event that our clients do appear, we require copies of the relevant chapters immediately.

To our knowledge, your client still intends to send the Book today, 9 July 2009. Please provide the information requested by return and in any event by no later than **2.30pm today** unless you confirm to us that your client undertakes not proceed with sending the Book to print without first giving our clients 3 business days notice via this firm

We continue to reserve all of our clients' rights.

Yours faithfully

SCHILLINGS

FARRER&Co

Schillings
DX 89265 Soho Square 1

Your reference	JK/JO/an/O0042/008
Our reference	JCP/
Direct telephone	020 7917 7217
Direct facsimile	020 7405 2296
Direct email	jcp@farrer.co.uk

6 July 2009

By fax and DX – 020 7034 9200

Dear Sirs

Osbourne v Beautiful Books

Thank you for your letter of 2 July sent at 9.42 pm demanding a response by 5 pm on Friday.

As we confirmed on Friday when we spoke briefly, we are not greatly moved by your pursuit of this complaint on behalf of your clients when it is based on advancing matters which are plainly unsustainable and correspondence designed to threaten. Neither is our client. We do not consider it at all appropriate for our client to have to deal with matters which you – even if not your clients – will know not to be sustainable. This specifically applies to a number of the meanings you seek to construct out of the words in the relevant passages of the book.

Dealing with the first set of numbered points you raise, we comment as follows:

1. The book makes no such allegation and therefore carries no such defamatory meaning;

2. The book makes no such allegation. This passage deals with the division of contracts between Don Arden and Sharon Osbourne. It merely states that she could control (and "*be able to receive*") tour and merchandise income, as opposed to Arden who kept control of the production and publishing contracts. It does not state, as fact, that she did receive income, merely that she had the ability to. Even if it did, we do not accept that would be defamatory of an artist's manager, whatever the personal relationship between the manager and artist;

3. We are instructed Daisley and Kerslake will, if required, confirm this information. That said, it is much more of a comment on Sharon Osbourne's management of the band rather than a clear statement of her demand to fulfil her sexual appetite. You will have noted of course that the relevant passage refers to the demand being possibly in jest;

FARRER&Co

4. In respect of your claim that Sharon Osbourne acted improperly in the legal proceedings, no such allegations are made. As regards the financial consequences of a loss, it is not admitted that the words bear a defamatory meaning. A reader will not think less of your clients if they understood that your clients faced having to meet a liability of millions of pounds in the event of them losing the litigation and that this would make Sharon Osbourne and Don Arden broke. It must also be remembered that this is not said of your client today. Even she would presumably admit that she is wealthier today than at the relevant time;

5. It is not alleged that Ozzy Osbourne is (or was) a talent-less musician. Even if it did, that would be a matter for comment and it would not be necessary for Mr Machat (or anyone else for that matter) to have attended a rehearsal or writing session in order for him to hold a valid opinion;

6. The book suggests the knuckle story was, in Mr Machat's view, staged. It does not therefore carry any defamatory meaning;

7. It is not admitted that to make a financial payment to avoid deportation in the circumstances described is defamatory. We note no complaint is made about the fact that your client did in deed urinate on an historic war monument which, if untrue, would be a serious allegation. It is not untrue as the failure to complain acknowledges;

8. If required to, this allegation will be defended as true; and

9. The book does not make this allegation. The book actually says that a record company promotions man took drugs in Sharon Osbourne's office. That does not ordinarily suggest she was complicit. Frankly, given when this event occurred and the industry we are dealing with, no reasonable reader would be surprised to learn that a record company promotions manager had taken drugs. There is nothing in the passage which suggests your client condoned or was party to the promotions man's drug taking.

We are also instructed that the alleged factual inaccuracies are also ill-advised. Dealing with each of the seventeen points raised, albeit briefly:

1. Kelly Osbourne did know Margaux (it is not suggested that they are friends as of today);

FARRER&Co

Scillings
6 July 2009

2. The book doesn't allege Sharon Osbourne met Journey, but simply that she made her views on the band known;

3. You do not identify which dates are inaccurate. To the extent that some dates are inaccurate, that is not to say the event did not take place. We suspect your clients would have difficulty in remembering with precision dates of events taking place in the 1990's, not too mention the late 1970's and 1980's;

4. Mr Machat confirms the meeting took place, although he is prepared to concede it is possible the meeting took place other than in 1984. This can be amended to read "mid '80's";

5. Don Arden gave Mr Machat this information. Our client is happy to amend the book to read " *Don told me he kept the publishing ...* ";

6. The band was to be called Blizzard of Oz, although it is accepted in public Ozzy Osbourne only referred to himself on the billing;

7. Mr Machat confirms he was on the tour;

8. Mr Machat does not allege that he was with Ozzy Osbourne the next day following the incident itself. The book refers to the day after the "*Alamo drama*", meaning after the drama was over, the drama lasting for longer than the day of the incident itself;

9. Denied. It is not suggested that there is a current rapport or friendship;

10. Denied. Mr Machat confirms this did happen;

11. One of our client's directors, Simon Petherick, has listened to the tape recording made in 2000. He is satisfied that it is clear from the tape that at the time of the recording Don Arden was self-evidently of sound mind;

12. This is not alleged. When Mr Machat met Don Arden as mentioned in the book, the latter was in a one bedroom flat. Only afterwards, once Sharon Osbourne was reconciled with her father, did she move him to a larger apartment;

13. Mr Machat confirms he was present;

FARDM1-1333962.1

FARRER&Co

14. The reference is not to Myron Roth being Ozzy Osbourne's lawyer, nor does it say in the book he was Sony's lawyer;

15. Mr Machat stands by the accuracy of the information;

16. Mr Machat has confirmed that Randy Rhodes did work as a session musician; and

17. Denied. Mr Machat confirms the book is accurate.

There is no claim that the book is authorised by your clients. Why would it? It is not about your clients, other than in passing.

Undertakings

We comment as follows:

1. See above with regard to the individual allegations complained of.

2. Should it become necessary, the requisite undertakings will be given.

3. We are taking our client's instructions. Unless there are references to your clients in other parts of the book, our client will not disclose to you the remainder of the book as it will not concern your clients. If there is to be any further disclosure, it will only be of the relevant references.

4. We do not accept you are entitled to this information.

5. Our client has not entered into any syndication agreement with a third party.

We confirm that we are instructed to act on behalf of all the directors of Beautiful Books and have instructions to accept service on their behalf. However, we fail to see why you would need to bring them in as Defendants, other than deploying this as some form of "frightener" tactic. It is the company that is providing the answers, not the individual directors, and it is the company that is the publisher. Your threat is unattractive and transparent.

FARRER&Co

Scillings
6 July 2009

We reserve our client's position on the question of costs on this threatened course of action.

We are taking instructions on whether we are also instructed to act on behalf of Mr Machat.

As for *Reynolds*, we are pleased to note that you acknowledge the public interest in the matters contained within the book. The question of the chronology is a matter to be litigated on another day and we fully reserve our client's rights on this issue.

We also confirm that our client will comply with its disclosure obligations.

Yours faithfully

other defamatory allegations concerning our clients will be removed from the Book.

2. In the absence of your undertaking we require Beautiful Books formal written undertaking that it fully intends in subsequent proceedings for libel (which will inevitably follow) to rely solely on the defence of justification and that Beautiful Books intends to prove the truth of identified defamatory allegations made concerning our clients to be true and that a Director of Beautiful Books is prepared to substantiate any claim of justification with a witness statement on Oath that he or she believes the same to be true and will provide the basis for such belief. This relates to all of the defamatory allegations in the Book including Chapter 4 of the Book.

3. We require your confirmation that these are no other references to our clients in the Book. If there are further references to our clients we require these to be provided by 3.00 pm on Thursday 16 October 2008. We also repeat our request for a copy of the manuscript of the Book by this time.

4. We require your clients undertaking to remove our clients from the cover artwork of the Book.

5. It is clear from your client's conduct that advance copies of the Book have been provided to third parties for review including Jay Williams. Please confirm how many advance copies of the original copy of the Book have been distributed, to whom and when.

We require your response to the above matters as a matter of urgency and in any event by no later than **3.00 pm today Thursday 16 October 2008**. In the absence of such undertakings we will advise our client to make an application for a pre-publication restraining order to prevent publication of the defamatory allegations.

If such application is necessary, then it will clearly be appropriate to move the court at short notice given your assertion that your client intends to proceed with the printing process as of Friday this week and refusal to confirm the actual date when the Book will go into production at the printers.

In the event that your client requires any further time to respond such request can only be considered provided your client agrees to provide an interim

5

Schillings
LAWYERS

undertaking that your client will not take any further steps to progress publication of the Book, unless it has first given our clients through this office at least 3 clear business days notice of its intention to proceed with publishing the Book.

We also require your confirmation that your client will retain all copies of the Book and all documents that are relevant to the dispute including but not limited to emails, distribution lists, manuscripts and drafts of the Book as well as all documents that show what steps have been taken to verify the allegations in the Book.

We await your reply by the deadline and continue to reserve all of our clients' rights.

Yours faithfully

SCHILLINGS

FARRER&Co

Schillings
Solicitors
DX 89265 (Soho Square 1)

Your reference   JK/JO/an/00042/008
Our reference   JCP/kp
Direct telephone   020 7917 7217
Direct facsimile   020 7405 2296
Direct email   jcp@farrer.co.uk

16 October 2008

By Fax: 020 7034 9200
By Post

Dear Sirs

Your clients: Sharon and Ozzy Osbourne
Our client: Beautiful Books Limited

Thank you for your letter of this morning.

We are in the process of taking instructions from our client but this is being hindered by the fact that the person from whom we are taking our instructions is overseas. It is not therefore possible to respond substantively to your letter by the deadline you give.

We are therefore instructed to confirm that our client will not take any further steps to progress publication of the Book subject to giving your clients, via your office, three clear business days' notice of our client's intention to proceed with publishing the Book.

We fully reserve our client's rights in relation to all those matters raised in your letter of today's date pending our client being in a position to respond substantively to the points you raise.

Yours faithfully

Farrer & Co LLP 66 Lincoln's Inn Fields London WC2A 3LH **Telephone** +44 (0)20 7242 2022 **Facsimile** +44 (0)20 7242 9899
DX 32 Chancery Lane **Website** www.farrer.co.uk

Farrer & Co LLP is a limited liability partnership registered in England and Wales, registered number OC323570, and is regulated by the Solicitors Regulation Authority. FARDM1-969331.1
A list of the members of the LLP is displayed at the above address, together with a list of those non-members who are designated as partners.

FARRER&Co

Schillings
Solicitors
DX 89265 (Soho Square 1)

Your reference	JK/JO/an/00042/008
Our reference	JCP/MXP/66155/1
Direct telephone	020 7917 7217
Direct facsimile	020 7405 2296
Direct email	jcp@farrer.co.uk

24 October 2008

By Fax: 020 7034 9200
By Post

Dear Sirs

Your clients: Sharon and Ozzy Osbourne
Our client: Beautiful Books Limited

We refer to your letter of yesterday.

We understand from our client that it has postponed its plans to publish the Book while it investigates this matter further and considers whether it intends to proceed with publication. We confirm that no copies of the Book are currently being used for sales and promotional purposes and that any reference to the Book has been removed from our client's website. We are also instructed to confirm that our client will continue to abide by its undertaking and not take any steps to progress publication of the Book subject to giving your clients, via your office, three clear business days' notice of our client's intention to proceed with publication.

As for the supply of the manuscript, we and our client are not prepared to disclose this to you. It is unnecessary to do so given our client is prepared to continue with its present undertaking as set out above.

For the time being we do not intend to respond to the balance of your letter. By not responding you and your clients should not assume that what is set out in it is accepted. There are a number of matters which we would challenge. For the avoidance of doubt, we fully reserve our client's rights in relation to all those matters raised in your letter.

Yours faithfully

Ferrer & Co

Farrer & Co LLP 66 Lincoln's Inn Fields London WC2A 3LH Telephone +44 (0)20 7242 2022 Facsimile +44 (0)20 7242 9899
DX 32 Chancery Lane Website www.farrer.co.uk

Farrer & Co LLP is a limited liability partnership registered in England and Wales, registered number OC323570, and is regulated by the Solicitors Regulation Authority. FARDM1-974717.1
A list of the members of the LLP is displayed at the above address, together with a list of those non-members who are designated as partners.

RECORD OF ATTENDANCE

Client	Beautiful Books Limited	Date	13 October 2008
Matter	Ozzy Osbourne/Sharon Osbourne	Ref	JCP/MXP

JCP and MXP meeting with Steven Machat regarding the letter from Schillings dated 10 October 2008.

SM started by saying that because he was a lawyer, he believed that Sharon Osbourne (SO) was always quite intimidated by him. He was believable and he thought this scared her. On the other hand he had always got on quite well with OO (at least until SO met him).

JCP said he wanted to go through each of the 11 allegations Schillings have identified and get some further background on these from SM. Once they had done this, they would need to speak to Simon Petherick and the insurers tomorrow. At the moment, SM was indemnified by his insurer. He had £2 million in cover. Although £2 million might sound a lot, JCP warned that if this matter went to trial, the £2 million would get eaten up very quickly. If they fought this and lost, it was possible that the liability would go over £2 million, in which case SM and Beautiful Books would be liable for any amount over the £2 million.

SM's background

SM explained that he was sworn into the Tennessee Bar in 1976, the Californian Bar in August 1977 and the New York Bar in February 1978. As he explains in his book, he had his licence suspended in California because he got into a dispute with a Japanese company and was accused of taking money. This happened at a time when his family was a mess and his daughter was facing serious addiction problems. She was in and out of institutions. He received a two year suspension from the California Bar, and although he passed all his re-admittance tests after the two years, he never applied to be readmitted. [Subsequent search suggests SM made bankrupt.]

SM explained that he had worked as a manger for recording artists for the last 20 years. He had done everything from producing movies and films to getting involved in political campaigns. He had also passed the CPA (the accountancy exam in the US) when he was an undergraduate. JCP asked whether there was any argument that SM had breached the confident of OO and SO by writing the book. SM said he was never OO's or SO's lawyer. Whilst SM's father had been hired by Don Arden (DA) to give business and legal advice, SM was hired by DA to run the business affairs for Jet Records in LA. He was not DA's lawyer — he never got paid for any legal advice. They hired external lawyers to give legal advice. He certainly did not owe SO any duties. JCP said that this was potentially a thin line.

The allegations

JCP explained that there was a significant difference in libel law between the UK and the US. It was far more claimant friendly in this country. The burden was on the publisher to prove the allegation was true, rather than on the Claimant to prove the allegation was untrue.

SM asked whether SO would ultimately have to come to Court and give evidence. JCP explained that whilst she would have to do this if the matter ultimately went to trial, that would only be at the very end of the proceedings. We would need, particularly given the threat of an injunction, to have all our cards in a row well before then.

Taking each of the allegations in turn:

1. SO tried to bribe SM into releasing Ozzy Osbourne (OO) from a recording contract

This allegation is on page 127 of the book.

JCP explained that SO and OO were complaining the allegation was defamatory on the basis it meant SO had tried to bribe SM into releasing OO from the contract. SM said SO was not trying to bribe him when she offered him the $500,000. He doubted there was even $500,000 in the case. She was proposing a business transaction. In effect, she was trying to fire him. She was acting as if she was entitled to do that. The reality of course was that she was not entitled to do that because SM worked for DA (not for SO). SM said that SO could not believe he did not take the money.

SM confirmed that this was an accurate record of the conversation. It took place in 1984 in his old office on the 30th floor of 1501 Broadway. SM specifically remembered SO telling him that DA would "fuck" him over.

SM said he did not keep a note of the conversation. However, he had an "insane memory" and he kept all of this information in his head. He said that his ex-wife, Lisa Machat (LM), would be able to confirm this story. SM knew that his father had told her that she should tell SM to take the money because everyone "needed something to fall back on". SM said that he was still in touch with LM. In fact he was still paying her money and he was confident that she would help back up this story.

SM said that Michael Parento (MP) (his secretary at the time) would have witnessed the incident. SM and MP had not been in touch in years and SM thought MP had possibly have died of AIDS.

SM believed that they were partners in Princess Productions. SM made it quite clear that his relationship was with her father, DA

JCP asked for further information about Princess Productions Inc. SM explained that it was incorporated in Cook County in Nevada in 1981. It was meant to be SM and SO taking care of their fathers. It was to be owned by SO and SM, but SM never in fact issued the stock. It was incorporated, as SM explains in his book, for the sole purpose of putting OO's contracts into the company so that CBS could not cross-collateralise

2

them against Jet Records. SO was the secretary and president, while SM was the treasurer and vice-president.

SM said that he did not have any documentation relating to Princess Productions. However, he thought that DA's former mistress, Meredith Goodwin, would be able to give chapter and verse on this.

2. SO bleeds OO for commissions

This allegation is on page 129 of the book.

It was agreed that Schillings had misquoted the book. Page 129 says "now Sharon would be able to bleed Ozzy for commissions ...". SM was simply saying that SO had an opportunity to do it, not that she actually did it.

JCP said he knew how to respond to this.

As an aside, SM said that SO had got Bob Daisley (BD) and Les Kerslake (LK) to sue DA for royalties, but when she ultimately got the contracts she did exactly the same to them.

3. SO required sexual behaviour from her road crew

This allegation is on page 137 of the book.

SM said that it was possible to get evidence from BD and LK, as well as John Freund (JF) Tom Brackey (TB). JF and TB had acted for BD and LK in their litigation against SO and they knew the whole story. SM knew JF and TB well. He had been contacted by them in around 2000 when they asked him to help prepare BD and LK's case against SO.

SM explained that whilst TB and JF did not have sex with SO, they had plenty of stories they had been told by BD and LK. They had also taken DA's original testimony.

JF's direct line was 001 310-247-2165 while TB's direct line was 001 310-804-7655. JF's email was johnfreund@freundandbrackey.com

William Mamone (WM) who was part of the road crew would also be a good person to speak to about this – SM knew that SO had had sex with WM. Indeed, he had a very funny story about how quick SO was to undo a man's zipper. WM's telephone number was 001 310-650-4488. His e-mail was williammamone@hotmail.com

SM said that Glen Hughes and Gary Moore would also be able to assist. JCP queried whether these people would want to come to Court. SM queried whether we could play bluff, but JCP explained that this would only get them so far. We certainly could not tell a Court later this week that any of these witnesses would give evidence supporting our version of events if that was not the case.

SM said that his ex-wife, LM, would also be able to give evidence about this allegation. SM said that LM and SO used to be good friends and SO would tell LM about all the people she had sex with. In fact, SM knew that SO had told LM that she was worried that her oldest child was not in fact OO's child.

JCP asked whether BD and LK (and any other witnesses) could give evidence about the relevant period. SM said that it was exactly this period when they would have been involved.

JCP said he was sure that Schillings would definitely want this allegation removed from the book. It was therefore potentially a real problem area. The sentence on page 137 was only one line ("Plus Sharon required sexual behaviour with her road crew at her whim") and he therefore queried whether it was necessary. We were going to need to produce people to make it stand up. If we only produced one person, or even possibly two, that was not going to be enough. You would want to produce five to six people who could give evidence about the relevant time. If we were going to stand behind this allegation, we would need witnesses to say it was true and that they were there.

SM confirmed that he was not particularly worried if this allegation came out of the book. It was agreed that it was more important to get the book out.

SM said that he in fact did not put in the sentence about her having sex with the road crew. This must have been put in by his co-author.

4. SO was a sexual predator of teenage boys

This allegation is on page 140 of the book.

SM explained that in his eyes under age meant under 16, although technically it could mean under 18. SM said that SO used to do this to make her father mad.

SM recalled that SO had once been arrested in Beverly Hills. She had been out partying with Britt Ekland and a woman called Doris Tyler (who was married to the clothes designer, Richard Tyler). SM got a telephone call in the middle of the night. SO had got picked up by the police two nights in a row. She had been arrested for lewd behaviour and disorderly conduct. It was not drunk driving because she got arrested just before she got into her car. SM did not go to the police station, but telephoned DA from his apartment and got DA to bail SO out. The bail was about $1,000.

SM said that SO used to pick up boys at a club in LA called the Rainbow Club. This was a rock and roll hang out. It was owned by Mario Valentino (MV), who also owned the Roxy Theatre (which was next door to the Rainbow Club). MV would be able to give evidence about SO and the young boys she got involved with. JCP asked why MV would want to get involved. SM said that parts of society quite liked him. He had always stood up for the Italians and on that basis MV might want to help.

JCP asked what the boys would be doing at the Rainbow Club. SM said that they were there to get drunk and get high. He did not know for sure, but he would not be surprised if money exchanged hands after the boys had sex with SO. JCP said that it would be very helpful to speak to MG. She might be able to point us to the mother of Andy William's road manager, who in turn could point them to her grandson.

JCP said that it seemed from SM's book that DA's girlfriend, MG, was in fact at the restaurant when the mother of Andy Williams' road manager told the story referred to on page 140.

JCP said Schillings would also want this allegation definitely removed from the book. He queried whether they could lose this section. He was concerned that they would not be able to get enough evidence to make it stand up. He certainly was not questioning what SM told him, but it was difficult to prove. It could only really stay in the book if we could justify it.

JCP asked who could give evidence about this allegation. SM said that MG, JF, TB and LA could all give helpful evidence. Additionally, WM would be able to help. He might even be able to help produce MV.

SM said that if push came to shove he was happy for this allegation to be taken out of the book.

5. SO is a racist who refused to do business with black people

This allegation is on page 141 of the book.

SM said that SO definitely hated black people. He recalled that SO would call him the "nigger manager". She could never understand how SM wanted to work with Richard Steckler and the likes of Eugene Record. SM said that he had always got on very well with black people and in fact had helped start Womad with Peter Gabriel. SO on the other hand hated black people.

SM said that Richard Steckler and Robert Richards could both attest to SO's racism. However, they were now quite old. LM could also confirm this allegation, although JCP questioned whether she could confirm that this was the reason Richard Steckler was fired by SO (given she was presumably not in the office during this period). SM said that she could however give evidence about how SO would ask her why SM was managing "niggers". This was in the late 1970s / early 1980s.

JCP asked whether Rod Temperton would help us. SM said that was very unlikely.

JCP asked whether there were any other examples of SO being racist. SM remembered SO calling him when she was drunk one night. This was on Friday 22 October 1999 when he was living at 1447 Sunset Plaza Drive. He remembered the date because his birthday was the next day, while LM's is on the 30 October. SM telephoned him and called him "nigger manager". She then asked why SM had sold "Ozzy Osbourne to death row …". This was the incident he referred to on page 276 of the book.

SM said that SO was completely lacking in class. In this respect, he knew that she had had her stomach stapled in 1981.

6. OO and SO acted fraudulently in the legal proceedings brought by BD and LK.

This allegation is in Chapter 21 of the book.

SM said that David Arden had told his story in the *News of the World*. JCP said that he was aware of that. He explained that the *NoW* had published two articles about SO last year after speaking to her brother, David Arden. There was one article about this particular allegation, which SO did not complain about. There was a second article, which SO did complain about, concerning an allegation that she was driving OO to an early grave by making him do back to back concerts and effectively working him too hard. It was said that SO was doing this because she needed the money – she was well known to have excessive spending habits. It was interesting at the time that SO did not sue about the first article regarding the family dispute.

Notwithstanding that, we would still have to prove the allegation was true. JCP said this was a difficult allegation for us to make because DA had obviously changed his story. Further, this allegation had previously been the subject of litigation in the US when BD and LK had brought their claims over there and it was likely a British Court would be reluctant to re-litigate this dispute again. SM said that BD and LK only ever lost on a procedural point. JCP said that may be true, but we would need to go back into all that detail. The Kerslake and Daisley litigation was a huge piece of litigation in its own right.

SM said that presumably they could get the bank accounts showing the payments. JCP questioned why JF and TB did not do that in the Kerslake and Daisley litigation. SM thought that JF and TB did not understand the difference between recording royalty payments and publishing royalty payments and that this had ended up costing them because they had drafted their pleadings poorly. In the end, not even the Judge understood what the difference was. Kerslake and Daisley were also struggling to fund the litigation.

JCP said it would be very useful to speak to JF and TB. He needed a summary of what the case was about and why it was thrown out of Court. We would need to get inside that information before we could consider running it as a defence. We would need to have a good case proving that SO had paid money to her father for him to change his testimony.

SM confirmed that he was happy for JCP to speak to JF and TB about the case. SM said it was probably best to speak to JF. At this point in the meeting, SM telephoned JF and introduced JCP. During this conversation, JF confirmed that MG's telephone number is 001 310-273-4104. According to JF, DA went in to their office after the litigation collapsed and apologised to them for changing his testimony.

SM said that he had heard that David Arden had AIDS. JCP said that he saw him only a year ago and he looked fine to him.

JCP asked SM to go through the meeting with DA. SM said that DA asked to meet with him. Although SO was trying to keep SM away from DA, DA wanted to clear everything up with SM. They met at a restaurant in LA and DA told SM he was broke and needed the money. He had also been desperate to see his grandchildren, which he had not done until after DA changed his evidence. He had seen them before DA's meeting with SM. DA explained to SM that he had accomplished everything he wanted. He had got to see his grandchildren. DA also said he was happy because he had been able to get some money from SO. SM recalled saying to DA that he was very happy he had been able to do that for DA. It was the Daisley / Kerslake case that got him that. DA and David Arden went on a salary after the Daisley/Kerslake case.

SM said that he felt he had done good. He walked away knowing that he had been able to get DA back with his grandchildren. DA asked him not to continue with the Daisley and Kerslake case and therefore SM walked away. SM had other projects lined up and therefore stepped aside.

JCP asked why DA had lost all his money. SM said that in 1978 DA had made an absolute fortune. He perhaps believed his own hype and the records started to stop. He spent a lot of money and eventually ended up with nothing. He also lost money from his accountant who had been stealing from him. It was thought that the accountant had taken somewhere in the region of $2 million. Don Arden finally found out about this and beat up the accountant. The accountant went to the police and somehow Don Arden got off, but David Arden went to jail. While the case was on, SO managed to get all the Jet Records contracts from DA. This was around 1986. DA never had any hit records again. DA used to live in the most luxurious apartment in Beverly Hills, but after he lost his money he had to move to MG's apartment in LA.

7. SO filed false allegations of assault against OO in order to obtain control over his accounts and money

This allegation is on page 278 of the book.

SM said that OO had been arrested in the UK. It was in the 1990's. This was information he had been told by DA. When OO had travelled to LA, OO met with DA and told him this.

JCP said we would need to prove that SO got OO arrested. It was not enough to say that DA told SM the story. He explained the repetition rule. This would be very difficult in this case. We would need the police officer and the custody records.

SM queried whether OO could give evidence. JCP said he was obviously not going to give evidence for us and would therefore not be required to give evidence until a trial. He certainly would not need to give evidence for a court hearing this week.

SM said that there were surely bank records and police records. JCP said that we would possibly be able to get our hands on the police records, but this would take time. We would need to know exactly when the incident took place and in any event we would need to get a Court Order first. He certainly did not doubt that the incident took place. He was simply telling SM that there was a difficulty in proving it.

SM said that surely we could get this information from the internet. JCP said that there may be rumours on the internet, but we could not get the actual police records from the internet. Even if we got that information, we would need to show that it was a false allegation made by SO.

JCP said it was possible, from a practical stand point, to easily take out the two paragraphs on page 278. SM said that he could always take this allegation out of the book and put it on his website. JCP said that was a matter ultimately for him.

8. SO and OO worshipped the occult and had a black magic altar on their tour bus

SM said that he had heard this story from Arthur Pollack. In SM's opinion, white magic was where you go to church and pray for the strength to fix your own problems. Black magic on the other hand was where you go to church and ask for someone to intervene. JCP said he did not think people would necessarily define black magic in that way.

SA explained that SO's entire "MO" in 1981 and 1982 was about worshipping the devil. All his songs were about it. There was even a picture of OO on an album cover brandishing a cross. SM said that the words "black Sabbath" actually meant devil worship. Black Sabbath in the Christian world means worship of the devil. OO had been sued in the US for devil worship · he had lost this case in the mid 1980s. Simon Petherick knew about the case.

JCP said he would do some research on the internet and also look at the books about Black Sabbath and OO.

JCP said that Arthur Pollack was now dead. He asked whether SM had a written report of this conversation. SM said all his information was in his head. He did not have any documents about this allegation, or indeed the other allegations.

JCP asked whether this allegation also applied to SO. You could not necessarily say SO was wording the occult just because OO was. SM said that he was told by SO that she had attended black magic ceremonies.

SM said that he did not necessarily care about this allegation and that if they wanted to remove it they should do. SM said that he knew that OO and SO had asked for sacrifices and met with a shaman. That particular allegation was not in the book. He knew this from his friend Charles. Charles' direct line was 001 323-463-5736. Charles was an Argentinean man, who had become a US Citizen by going to Vietnam.

JCP noted that there was another reference to the occult on page 295 of the book.

9. OO is a talentless musician with no musical credibility

SM said he did not say this in the book. He says that in 1981 OO was taking a lot of drugs. He does not say anywhere in the book that OO he has no talent. On page 133 he says that OO had a "lovely voice".

JCP knew that SO had admitted in the past to putting OO on the stage when he was not fit to perform.

10. OO misspelt his name on his knuckles

This allegation is on page 133 of the book.

JCP said he was not particularly worried about this allegation. It involved a meeting between SM and OO. He queried whether anyone would think less of OO because he could not spell his name on his knuckles. There seemed to be some evidence that OO

FARDM1-965571.1

spelt his name differently (at times he would call himself "Ozzie" and sometimes "Ozzy").

On page 134 SM says that "Ozzy wasn't as dumb as he looked".

11. OO was forced to make a financial payment in order to avoid being deported from the U.S.

SM said that this story was definitely true and was all over the internet. DA made a payment to the US government. SM did not know the exact figure, but he knows the payment was made. He had seen the figure quoted as being $10,000, but he was told by DA that it was "$100,000".

SM said that after OO was threatened with being deported, he went to see Morgan Mason (MM) (James Mason's son) who was at the time Nancy Reagan's secretary. They met at Le Dome restaurant in LA. This was back in 1982. He had had dinner with MM three nights before OO had been arrested because MM was dating LM's friend, Debbie He went to see MM again after OO was arrested who advised them to make a contribution to Nancy Regan's drug programme "Keep America Drug Free".

SM asked where the libel was. JCP agreed that there was a question mark about that. Assuming it was defamatory, he asked whether MM would still be around to give evidence. SM said he did not know. They were no longer in contact.

JCP asked whether OO would have known about the payment at the time. SM said almost certainly definitely.

At this point SM telephoned LM (direct line is 001 310-738-6838) and then WM.

Conclusion

JCP would contact SM tomorrow morning to update him. SM's e-mail was smachat@gmail.com. Said we thought they would probably need to drop some of the passages complained of for the sake of expediency. These were in relation to allegations 3, 4, 7 and possibly 8. SM said he was relaxed about these passages. He would not want to lose 6.

RECORD OF ATTENDANCE

Client	Beautiful Books	**Date**	20 October 2008
Matter	Sharon and Ozzy Ozbourne	**Ref**	JCP

JCP telephoning Robert Richards office at East End Management (001 818 7849002) spoke to Germaine, RR's assistant. She tried to put JCP through to RR's mobile but was unsuccessful. She said she would pass on JCP's number. Said we would email him in the meantime.

Telephoning and speaking to Jan Steckler (001 310 271 0651). Explained why JCP was calling. JS said she thought SO had a bit of a nerve to be complaining. RS had worked really hard with the groups. He had worked along with his affiliates including Alan Bernard. As far as JS was aware, nothing happened to get Heatwave to join Jet. She did not know why this had happened. She did not know whether this was because SO was racist. She did not have any knowledge of this. She said that SO was a "big fat pig". She was adamant and mean. She recalled that SO had had a fight with her father. She struggled to remember anything more.

She asked JCP if he knew of Sandy Bailey. Said we did not. She said that JCP should try and contact her. She knew everything.

She said that she was no longer in contact with her former husband. She only contacted him via his Californian office which was run by Bruce Kemper. Bruce's contact details were: Telephone number 001 310 838 3577 Fax: 001 310 838 2484.

Telephoning to speak to Bruce Kemper. Explained why we were calling. Confirmed that he ran the California office for Richard Steckler. Steckler now lived in Hong Kong. He was unable to find an email address for Steckler but he did have his telephone and fax numbers. These were: Telephone: 00 852 2119 1548 Fax: 00 852 2119 3388.

Faxing Richard Steckler.

Attending Robert Richards on his calling (01753 447 400).

Explained to RR why we were calling and in particular read out the passage from the book where the "nigger" reference was made.

RR said that he did not doubt that SO had made this comment, as between JCP and him. However, he could not attest to the quote. His recollection was that they were managing Heatwave. He was an employee of British American Management working along with Richard Steckler. BAM was part of the Columbus system as he recalled. Jet, he thought, was also part of the Columbus system. He did not recall what the issue was as to why Heatwave did not join Jet. Whether it would have been possible to have made a move from the Epic label to Jet he could not now recall. SO was an executive of Jet. She had a role in the decision making process at the label. He could not say that SO held racist views. Certainly however, her views held sway with Don Arden in terms of who the label would take on board. From his interaction with her and his knowledge of her, SO was at the time given a lot of latitude by DA to express herself. As a result, she was a fairly unchecked person. He doubted that SO had said the quote in front of Richard Steckler, but he wouldn't be surprised if she had said those words but he himself could not recall her saying them. He could not recall her saying any other statement which was evidence of her being a racist.

He tried to stay away from SO as much as possible. She was big on the campus at Jet Records. She was enjoying herself as the daughter of Don Arden. She was loud.

RR said that he was never very happy with SO. He recalled that she and her father had let her brother go to jail for her father's tax evasion. She had deep pockets, was litigious and very unpleasant. He thought it best to avoid the likes of her. He was happy to speak to JCP in the future if need be.

RECORD OF ATTENDANCE

Client	Beautiful Books Limited	**Date**	21 October 2008
Matter	Sharon and Ozzy Osbourne	**Ref**	JCP

JCP attending Richard Steckler on the telephone (00852 2119 1548). Said we were acting for Beautiful Books. It was publishing a book of Steve Machat's. Sharon Osbourne had made a complaint about a number of the allegations in the book concerning her. One of these included reference to her being racist. The book referred to a time when Jet were wanting to bring Heatwave on board. We understood RS was the manager of Heatwave. Apparently, SO was not going to have Heatwave on board and the book recorded that "she was nothing if not blunt": "niggers are not coming into my office. They are not for getting into business with, let alone managing: they are animals. I don't understand them and never wanna." Said that we wanted to know about the background to the attempts to get Heatwave on to the label and why it did not proceed.

RS said that he was the manager at the time for Heatwave. He was doing some work with Jet Records and had met Don Arden, Sharon Osbourne and David Arden. He had been told that there was a great interest in Heatwave and wished to get them on to the Jet Label. In fact, RS flew with Johnnie Wilder (then leader of the group) from London to New York. Jet Records had put them up at the Waldorf Astoria Hotel. They had met Don Arden. They had gone to an ELO concert in NY, ELO being with Jet Records and a big artist at the time.

They had had a meeting with Don Arden at which SO and DA had also been in attendance. Subsequently, RS had been told that Jet did not want to go ahead. He was never told the precise reason why they did not want to go ahead. He knew SM and his father, Marty. He recalled that he had been told by one of them that there was a lot more to it than that. Being a manager of black musicians, he was faced with this issue all the time during that period. It would not have shocked him if his group had not been signed up because of their colour. However, he could not say that he had been told that this was the reason why they had not signed Heatwave. He had found the Arden's bigoted in many ways from his dealings with them. They did not say directly to him that they were not going to sign his group because of their colour. However, they would not have surprised him if that had been the reason. He said that from memory, he thought that the issue that colour was the issue had been intimated to him by SM/MM from his conversations with them. However, in the business at the time, there were more times when bands were turned down than they were signed up. He was not unhappy with the situation given that CBS (then known as Columbus) resigned Heatwave so he wasn't disappointed. Columbus was very much into R&B/black music. He did not recall SM saying to him that Heatwave had been turned down because SO was racist.

RECORD OF ATTENDANCE

Client Beautiful Books Limited	**Date** 21 October 2008
Matter Sharon and Ozzy Ozbourne	**Ref** MXP

MXP telephoning Myron Roth on 310-899-1814. Explained that we acted for you and that you were about to publish a book written by Steven Machat which dealt with SM's career in the music industry over the past 30 years or so. Some sections of the book referred to SM's involvement with Sharon Osbourne ("Sharon") and Ozzy Osbourne ("Ozzy").

MXP explained that Sharon was complaining about some parts of the book. In particular, she was upset about the reference to a meeting in MR's office that took place on 12 May 1978. SM's recollection was that Sharon defecated on MR's desk when Electric Light Orchestra ("ELO") were about to sign a massive contract with CBS Records. MR confirmed that he was the head of CBS Records on the West Coast at the time and that he remembered signing ELO. Although his memory was hazy (given that the incident was 30 years ago), he recalled that Sharon's dog urinated on the carpet in his office by mistake. However, the dog certainly did not defecate on his desk. MR queried whether SM was even in the office at the time.

MR said "it sounds like quite a book" and asked whether his name appeared elsewhere in it. MXP explained that his name was mentioned in passing, but this was the only significant incident which involved him.

MXP asked MR about some of the other incidents involving Sharon and Ozzy. MR said that he did not have any knowledge of those incidents. He certainly could not say that Sharon held racist views or that she had sex with any members of her road crew. MR said he mostly dealt with Sharon's father, Don Arden, rather than Sharon. He was sorry he could not be more help, but he did not have a problem with Sharon and he did not therefore particularly want to get involved. In any event all of this was a long time ago.

MXP thanked MR for his time.

He did not have a great deal of time for the Ardens. He knew that the son had gone to jail for his dad, probably having something to do with non payment of revenue to the government. The family did not have the greatest of reputations in the world. He didn't want to go into detail since he had been a long time out of the business and there was no great interest for him, but all he would say was that he would not want them as relatives or friends.

Said the book contained a number of allegations about SO which he had taken offence to. One of these related to her having sex with the road crew. Another referred to her having a penchant for teenage boys. RS said he knew nothing about teenage boys but, without wishing to be flippant, everyone was having sex on the road. It wasn't known as sex, drugs and rock and roll for nothing. He could well image SO being unhappy with adverse publicity.

SOLICITORS

ʰRussell

Regency House
1-4 Warwick Street
London W1B 5LJ

TEL: +44(0)20 7439 8692
FAX: +44(0)20 7494 3582
EMAIL: media@russells.co.uk
WEB: www.russellslaw.co.uk

DX: 37249 Piccadilly 1

Simon Petherwick
Beautiful Books
36-38 Glasshouse Street
London W1B 5DL

BY POST & BY E-MAIL: simon@beautiful-books.co.uk

Dear Simon

RE: GODS & GANGSTERS – STEVEN MACHET

As discussed during our telephone conversation last week, I have now had the opportunity of reviewing the draft of the above-named book which you sent to me by e-mail on 15 May and am now in a position to provide you with the appropriate legal report. As I mentioned to you, I have not confined my advice to potential defamatory problems as I think that there are two other issues which ought to be considered which I deal with below, namely:-

1. **CLIENT ATTORNEY PRIVILEGE** - (excuse the American but Steven is a registered US attorney)

   Whilst I am not an expert on the USA bar rules (or indeed the individual state bar rules), the issue of client attorney privilege is the same as it is here. US attorneys are under the same obligations as solicitors in this country and owe a duty to keep the affairs of their clients and former clients confidential except where disclosure is required or permitted by law. Any breach of this duty is actionable not only by the disciplinary authorities in the appropriate US state but, more importantly, the client or former clients themselves. Obviously it is open to the client or former client to permit disclosure but this would really need to be in writing to protect all parties concerned. It is therefore important when reviewing this draft manuscript that none of the disclosures contained were given to Steven when acting in his capacity as an attorney and for that purpose only.

2. **CONFIDENTIALITY - GENERAL**

   In addition to the client attorney privilege, it is evident that Steven has also acted in a managerial capacity on behalf of several of his clients. As a manger he owes a fiduciary duty to his artists and that includes, amongst other things, a common law duty of confidentiality. Again therefore, where Steven's knowledge has been solely derived from acting in his capacity as a manager, it will be important to ensure that the relevant artist has given the consent to the disclosure.

PARTNERS: A.J.English, B.K.Howard, C.D.Organ, M.E.Sinnott, S.M.Tregear, S.M.Esplen, G.A.Maude, P.W.Smith, C.A.Gossage, J.P.Reid. CONSULTANTS: A.D.Russell E.J.Wyllie
This firm does not accept service of proceedings by email.
Regulated by the Solicitors Regulation Authority.

It follows from the above that where the information is already in the public domain it cannot be a breach of either of these duties and so if at all possible it is important to ascertain what information is truly confidential and what is not. I make this observation since, as you will see from the libel report below, there have been numerous books and articles published concerning many of the individuals to whom Steven refers and I suspect, but do not know, that such things as, for example, the financial terms of the ELO deal, are and have been in the public domain for some time. It is however something which Steven will need to address.

3. **LIBEL**

As you are aware from my previous report, a statement is defamatory if it would be likely to lower the reputation of the person about whom it is made (all be understood to be referring to) in the eyes of the average reader. For legal purposes a company is treated as a separate legal person.

On the face of it, the draft manuscript contains numerous defamatory statements (as to which see the schedule annexed to this letter) which principally relate to the following allegations, namely:-

(i) Fraud/corruption

(ii) Drug use and abuse

(iii) Dishonesty – of a more general nature.

(iv) Racism

(v) Sexuality

The two principal defences to any libel complaint are:-

(a) Justification (truth)

This is complete defence to any complaint. However, it is up to the publisher/author to demonstrate that what has been published is true on the balance of probabilities based upon admissible evidence. To rely upon allegations being previously published is not in itself evidence of the truth but in this case may be an indication of it given the wide spread publicity that has been given to many of the allegations previously particularly with regard to corruption and drug abuse.

(b) Fair comment

This applies when the defamatory allegations take the form of comment. The defence applies where comment can be shown to be within the spectrum of views someone could reasonably hold based on facts which can be shown by the author/publisher to be true.

Unlike the situation in other areas of civil, the dead cannot sue for libel. Accordingly, I have not included in my report any references to the following:-

a) The Grandmother – Mrs Golden

b)   Grandpa Charlie

c)   Sam Cooke

d)   Don Arden

e)   Artie Mogull

f)   Morris Levy

g)   Neil Bogart

all of whom I believe to be deceased.

It is also likely that certain individuals about whom defamatory comments have been made would be unlikely to complain for various reasons due to not wanting to offend the author or more likely not wishing to have their personal life exposed in a Court of law. My principal concern here is in relation to the various allegations made against Sharon Osbourne. The draft manuscript comes over as being a particularly damming inditement of her earlier character which she may now wish to try and disown given her current success and high profile derived from the X Factor. She is certainly someone who could afford to bring a libel action but whether she would have the inclination to do so obviously remains to be seen. Obviously many of the matters which are referred to in this draft manuscript are within Steven's first-hand knowledge and the comments contained in this letter and the schedule are made on the basis that Steven can provide first-hand evidence of the various matters and would be available to assist in dealing with any relevant complaint.

As I mentioned to you, I think it would be useful for you or someone in your company to review, in particular, Sharon Osbourne's autobiography in order to see as to whether she admits to the sort of conduct which Steven is accusing her of as obviously if she does then there is the defence of justification. Outside of that source, I am also aware of the several books which have made similar allegations both in respect of corruption and drug abuse where no action has been taken and as stated above, whilst this is no admissible evidence of justification, it is perhaps indicative of whether a person is likely to sue or not.

Clearly, a decision will need to be made regarding the appropriate level of commercial risk to be taken in connection with this book as by its very nature publication cannot be made risk free.

No doubt once you have considered the above and the attached schedule, we can discuss the matter further.

With all best wishes.

Yours sincerely

BRIAN HOWARD

Direct Litigation Fax: 020 7287 0314

Enc

FARRER&Co

Schillings
Solicitors
DX 89265 (Soho Square 1)

26 June 2009

Your reference	JK/JO/an/00042/008
Our reference	JCP/MXP/vs
Direct telephone	020 7917 7217
Direct facsimile	020 7405 2296
Direct email	jcp@farrer.co.uk

By Fax: 020 7034 9200
By Post

Dear Sirs

Your clients: Sharon and Ozzy Osbourne
Our client: Beautiful Books Limited

We refer to our letter of 18 June 2009 in which we promised you a response to the detailed matters raised in your letter of 17 June 2009 by the close of business today. We have now taken our client's instructions and are in a position to respond.

Our client's undertaking

As we advised you in our letter of 18 June 2009, our client's website makes clear that our client is not intending to publish "*Gods, Gangsters and Honour*" ("the Book") until 6 August 2009. We have also advised you (see our letter of 22 June 2009) that in light of this publication date, the print date for the book is 9 July 2009. Bearing this in mind, any suggestion that our client has breached its undertaking to your clients is strongly rejected.

In any event, your assertion that our client has in some way breached its undertaking to your clients seems to be based on out of date material contained on the website, http://machatsgodsandgangsters.com/home/html. This website has nothing to do with our client and, in fact, we understand it has now been removed from the internet. We would add that it is our client's opinion that the Book it intends to publish on 6 August 2009 is a wholly different book to "*Gods and Gangsters*" in relation to which our client gave its undertaking. Our client is promoting the Book very much as a new book and in this regard you will note from our client's website that the Book has a different title, ISBN and cover.

The Book

We have reviewed the manuscript of the Book and whilst there are certainly references to your clients in it, it is not an account of events based around your clients and Don Arden. Rather it is Mr

Farrer & Co LLP 66 Lincoln's Inn Fields London WC2A 3LH Telephone +44 (0)20 7242 2022 Facsimile +44 (0)20 7242 9899
DX 32 Chancery Lane Website www.farrer.co.uk
Farrer & Co LLP is a limited liability partnership registered in England and Wales, registered number OC323570, and is regulated by the Solicitors Regulation Authority. FARDM1-1327328.2

FARRER&Co

Schillings
26 June 2009

Machat's account of his career and the events to which he was a party. Your clients' involvement in Mr Machat's career is, of course, limited and this is reflected in the fact that your clients only appear in two chapters of the Book.

Your letter of 17 June 2009 also rather assumes that the Book remains unaltered from the version seen by you and your client last autumn. This is not the case. Substantial amendments have been made and account taken of your clients' objections. Our client does not consider that your client should now have any concerns.

We are content that there is nothing in the Book that is defamatory of your clients unless capable of justification and in this respect our client and Mr Machat are satisfied that the references to your clients are true. Notwithstanding this, our client is prepared to provide you with two chapters of the Book which mention your clients. Copies of those two chapters will be sent to you next week.

In light of the print date of the book (ie 9 July 2009) your clients will suffer absolutely no prejudice waiting until next week to see the two chapters that mention your client. Please note that should your clients proceed with an application for a pre-publication restraining order to prevent publication of the Book (or indeed any part of the Book) our client will submit evidence confirming its intention to rely upon the defence of justification and detail as necessary the evidence it intends to rely upon supported by statements of truth. We rely upon this letter on the question of costs, should you proceed with an application.

Please would you confirm that your clients will provide the necessary cross undertaking in damages. We understand that such an undertaking would not be less than £500,000.

In the circumstances, we do not agree that your clients are entitled to bring any claim whatsoever against our client arising out of the publication of the Book. In the event you do issue proceedings against our client, you should be aware that our client will defend such proceedings vigorously and will seek to recover its legal costs from your clients.

In relation to the demands numbered 1-8 beginning on page 3 of your letter of 17 June 2009, we respond as follows:

1.   No undertaking (or apology) will be provided.

FARRER&Co

Schillings
26 June 2009

2 & 3.   We confirm that the only references to your clients are in the two chapters which we will send to you next week.

4.   You will note from our client's website that the cover of the Book is different to the cover of "*Gods and Gangsters*" and indeed your clients are not featured on it. The cover in fact is only a photograph of Mr Machat. In the circumstances, it is not necessary to provide the undertaking you have requested.

5.   Since your clients cannot have any complaint about the Book, there is no need to address the issue of serialisation.

6 & 7.   We do not accept that you are entitled to this information, particularly bearing in mind what we say above;

8.   See above. This request would also appear to be pre-mature given that you and your clients do not know what you are complaining about and have not, as a consequence, identified those passages which your clients claim to be defamatory and untrue.

For the avoidance of doubt, it is our client's intention to proceed with publication of the Book on 6 August 2009. In the meantime, all of our client's rights remain reserved.

Yours faithfully

Schillings
Lawyers

PRIVATE AND CONFIDENTIAL
Farrer & Co
66 Lincolns Inn Fields
London
WC2A 3 LH

By facsimile: 020 7406 2296

Our Ref: JK/JO/an/O0042/008
Your ref: JCP/MXP/86155/1
24 June 2009

Dear Sirs

SHARON AND OZZY OSBOURNE

We refer to your letter dated 23 June 2009.

We note that your client's response will be provided on Friday 26 June 2009.

In the absence of a satisfactory response and provision of the undertaking and information sought, we will advise our clients to apply for a pre-publication restraining order.

We continue to reserve all of our clients' rights.

Yours faithfully

SCHILLINGS

SCHILLINGS 41 Bedford Square, London WC1B 3HX
Tel 020 7034 9000 · Fax 020 7034 9200
Email legal@schillings.co.uk · Online www.schillings.co.uk · DX Number 89265 (Soho Square 1)

Regulated by the Solicitors Regulation Authority

286426_1

FARRER&Co

Schillings
DX 89265
Soho Square 1

23 June 2009

Your reference   JK/JO/an/O0042/008
Our reference   JCP/MXP/ms/66155/1
Direct telephone   020 7917 7217
Direct facsimile   020 7405 2296
Direct email   jcp@farrer.co.uk

By Fax: 020 7034 9200
By DX

Dear Sirs

Your clients: Sharon and Ozzy Osbourne
Our client: Beautiful Books Limited

We refer to your letter of yesterday, received by us at 6.21pm.

As we have advised you, our client is currently taking advice in relation to this matter and should be in a position to provide its detailed response to your letter of 17 June 2009 by the close of business on Friday, 26 June 2009, no sooner. Given the print date for "*Gods, Gangsters & Honour*" is 9 July 2009, your clients will suffer absolutely no prejudice waiting another day for our client's response.

Please note that in the event your clients decide to pursue an application for a pre-publication restraining order, we reserve our client's right to bring this letter to the Court's attention on the issue of costs.

Yours faithfully

rrer & Co LLP 66 Lincoln's Inn Fields London WC2A 3LH Telephone +44 (0)20 7242 2022 Facsimile +44 (0)20 7242 9899
32 Chancery Lane **Website** www.farrer.co.uk

rer & Co LLP is a limited liability partnership registered in England and Wales, registered number OC323570, and is regulated by the Solicitors Regulation Authority. FARDM1-1324574.1
st of the members of the LLP is displayed at the above address, together with a list of those non-members who are designated as partners.

Lawyers

<u>**PRIVATE AND CONFIDENTIAL**</u>
Farrer & Co
66 Lincolns Inn Fields
London
WC2A 3 LH

By facsimile: 020 7405 2296

Our Ref: JK/JO/an/O0042/008
Your ref: JCP/MXP/66155/1
22 June 2009

Dear Sirs

SHARON AND OZZY OSBOURNE

We refer to your letter of today's date.

We note that the print date for the Book is 9 July 2009. You give no reason as to why your client is unable to provide a substantive reply to our letter until the end of this week. This is unacceptable.

Our client is prepared to grant a short extension of time for your client to provide its substantive response to our letter dated 17 June 2009 to **2.00 pm on Thursday 25 June 2009**. This will provide your client with over a week within which to provide its substantive response which, given you have been previously instructed in relation to this matter, is ample time to deal with this issue.

In the absence of the requested undertakings and information by **2.00 pm on Thursday 25 June 2009**, we will advise our client to pursue an application for a pre-publication restraining order to prevent publication of the offending chapters.

We await your reply as a matter of urgency and reserve all of our client's rights.

Yours faithfully

SCHILLINGS

SCHILLINGS 41 Bedford Square, London WC1B 3HX
Tel 020 7034 9000 · Fax 020 7034 9200
Email legal@schillings.co.uk · Online www.schillings.co.uk · DX Number 89265 (Soho Square 1)

Regulated by the Solicitors Regulation Authority

294476_2

FARRER&Co

Schillings
Solicitors
DX 89265 (Soho Square 1)

Your reference	JK/JO/an/00042/008
Our reference	JCP/MXP/vs
Direct telephone	020 7917 7217
Direct facsimile	020 7405 2296
Direct email	jcp@farrer.co.uk

22 June 2009

By Fax: 020 7034 9200
By Post

Dear Sirs

Your clients: Sharon and Ozzy Osbourne
Our client: Beautiful Books Limited

We refer to your letter of 19 June 2009.

We confirm that the print date for *"Gods, Gangsters & Honour"* is 9 July 2009 (over two weeks away).

We hope to provide you with our client's detailed response by the close of business on Friday, 26 June 2009. We shall inform you as soon as possible if we are not able to meet that deadline.

Yours faithfully

Farrer & Co

Farrer & Co LLP 66 Lincoln's Inn Fields London WC2A 3LH Telephone +44 (0)20 7242 2022 Facsimile +44 (0)20 7242 9899
DX 32 Chancery Lane Website www.farrer.co.uk
Farrer & Co LLP is a limited liability partnership registered in England and Wales, registered number OC323570, and is regulated by the Solicitors Regulation Authority. FARDM1-1323259.1

41 Bedford Square
London
WC1B 3HX
Tel no: +44(0)20 7034 9000
Fax no: +44(0)20 7034 9200
Legal@schillings.co.uk
www.schillings.co.uk

To	Farrer & Co		
/	Julian Pike		
From	Schillings	**Fax**	020 7405 2296
Pages	10	**(Inclusive)**	**Date** 17 June 2009
Re	Sharon and Ozzy Osbourne		

Please see attached.

Schillings
Lawyers

PRIVATE AND CONFIDENTIAL
Farrer & Co
66 Lincolns inn Fields
London
WC2A 3 LH

For the attention of Julian Pike
By facsimile, email and post
Facsimile: 020 7405 2296
Email: jcp@farrer.co.uk

Our Ref: JK/JO/an/O0042/008
Your ref: JCP/MXP/66155/1
17 June 2009

ON THE RECORD
URGENT - NOT FOR PUBLICATION

Dear Sirs

SHARON AND OZZY OSBOURNE

We act for Sharon and Ozzy Osbourne.

You act for Beautiful Books Limited ("Beautiful Books"). In the event that you are not acting for Beautiful Books any longer, please let us know by return and in any event by no later than 2.00pm on Thursday 18 June 2009. If we have not heard from you by that time we shall send a copy of this letter to Beautiful Books direct.

We have previously exchanged correspondence with you in connection with your client's plans to publish a book by Steven Machat ("the Book"). A copy of our letter to your client dated 10 October 2008 is enclosed. The Book, then called "Gods and Gangsters", now known as "Gods, Gangsters & Honour" is being advertised at Beautiful Books' website and is available for pre-order at several on line retailers including Amazon and Borders.

In your letter dated 24 October 2008 to this firm an undertaking was given on behalf of your client not to take any steps to progress publication of the Book

SCHILLINGS 41 Bedford Square, London WC1B 3HX
Tel 020 7034 9000 · Fax 020 7034 9200
Email legal@schillings.co.uk · Online www.schillings.co.uk · DX Number 89265 (Soho Square 1)

Regulated by the Solicitors Regulation Authority

Schillings
Lawyers

subject to giving our clients, via our office, three clear business days notice of your client's intention to proceed with publication. That undertaking has clearly been breached and our client's rights in respect of this breach are expressly reserved. Why has no notice been given to this firm?

It is not clear whether the allegations concerning our clients in the previous version of the Book are still included in the Book in full or in part. As previously noted, the chapters we have had sight of are littered with inaccuracies and are self evidently grossly defamatory of our clients. Publication of those chapters, or indeed any of the allegations concerning our clients, would be unlawful.

However, there are a number of factors which lead us to believe that our clients still feature in the Book:

1. At http://machatsgodsandgangsters.com/home.html the Book is still being advertised, and in what purports to be a current list of chapters at http://machatsgodsandgangsters.com/about_gg.html the chapters relating to our clients remain listed.

2. The increase in the number of pages to 484 from 380 indicates that the overall length of the Book has increased substantially.

3. Mr Machat has chosen to appear in a You Tube video (posted on the above website as an "advert") which features the introductory title "*Machat v Osbourne*" and contains footage of Mr Machat discussing our clients.

4. The Beautiful Books website boasts of "*appearances*" in the Book from, inter alia, Sharon Osbourne.

On this basis it appears highly likely that your client is proposing to publish at least some of the defamatory allegations in the Book.

Should the defamatory allegations previously complained of or further defamatory allegations be included in the Book, our clients are clearly entitled to pursue a claim for damages in relation to any publication of the Book, and are entitled to:

1. The withdrawal of the offending allegations.

2. An apology in terms to be agreed with this firm.

3. An injunction preventing further publication of the allegations. An injunction preventing further use of our clients images in connection with the Book or promotion of the Book.

4. A Statement in Open Court to withdraw the libels.

5. Payment of our clients' legal costs.

279688_2

Schillings
Lawyers

6.   Payment of damages in relation to defamation.

7.   Payment of damages and/or an account of profits in relation to any infringement of our clients image rights.

In the event of publication, the defamatory statements will cause substantial damage to both of our clients. In addition to general libel damages, our clients are likely to suffer significant financial losses by way of lost broadcasting opportunities, sponsorship opportunities, and reduced ticket, record and merchandising sales. Such damages may run into hundreds of thousands of pounds Our clients will be entitled to recover such damages from Beautiful Books, including any special and aggravated damages caused by publication of the Book in any form – not least given the previous warnings which your client had had from this firm which will be given due prominence in any proceedings, should such proceedings prove to be necessary. Our clients will hold Beautiful Books liable for the republication of any of the allegations made in the Book by any third parties including any media reports of the Book (which given the subject matter and tone of the allegations are entirely foreseeable).

In the circumstances, we require from Beautiful Books as a matter of urgency and by no later than **2:00pm on Monday 22 June 2009**:

1.   An undertaking that Beautiful Books will immediately withdraw the offending allegations from the Book, together with any other references which are defamatory of our clients.

2.   Copies of all sections of the book to be provided to our client.

3.   Confirmation that there are no other references in the Book to our client.

4.   An undertaking that Beautiful Books will immediately remove our clients from the cover artwork, and all promotion of the book.

5.   An undertaking not exploit the Book in its current form including by way of serialisation. If the Book has already been offered for serialisation, we require a full list of who the serialisation rights have been offered to be provided by no later than 4.00pm on Wednesday 17 June 2009.

6.   A full list of the parties to whom the book has been sent including promotional copies to be provided by 4.00pm on Wednesday 17 June 2009.

7.   An undertaking to provide this firm by 4.00pm on Wednesday 17 June 2009 with:

    (a)   A full copy of the manuscript.
    (b)   Details of all pre-orders.

Schillings
Lawyers

    (c)   Copies of any promotional material in relation to the Book.

    (d)   Details of any proposed print run and when the book is to be printed.

8.   In the absence of the undertaking sought in paragraph 1 above, we require Beautiful Books' formal written undertaking that it fully intends in subsequent proceedings for libel (which will inevitably follow) to rely solely upon the defence of justification and that Beautiful Books intends to prove the truth of identified defamatory allegations made concerning our clients to be true. If that is the case, any response to us must identify what allegations Beautiful Books intends to justify and confirm that a director of Beautiful Books is prepared to substantiate any claim of justification with a witness statement on oath that he or she believes the same to be true, and providing the basis for such belief[1].

In the event that we do not receive your client's undertaking by 2:00pm on Monday 22 June 2009 we will instruct our client to pursue an application for a pre-publication restraining order to prevent publication of the offending chapters.

We await your reply as a matter of urgency and reserve all of our clients' rights.

Yours faithfully

SCHILLINGS

---

[1] See *Sunderland Housing Company v Baines & others* [2006] EWHC 2359 (QB)

Schillings
Lawyers

PRIVATE AND CONFIDENTIAL
Beautiful Books Limited
36-38 Glasshouse Street
London W1B 5DL

For the attention of Simon Petherick
By email, by fax and by hand

Our Ref: JK/JO/an/O 0042/008
10 October 2008

ON THE RECORD
URGENT – NOT FOR PUBLICATION

Dear Sirs

SHARON AND OZZY OSBOURNE

We act for Sharon and Ozzy Osbourne.

We have been instructed that Beautiful Books Limited ("Beautiful Books") plan to publish a book titled *"Gods and Gangsters"* by Steven Machat on 30th October 2008 ("the Book"). The Book is advertised at Beautiful Books' website and is available for pre-order at several on line retailers including Amazon and Borders.

Last night, at 17.42, copies of chapter 11 and 21 of the Book were emailed to our clients' office by your Publisher, Mr Simon Petherick.

The two chapters of the Book which we have had sight of focus upon our clients, who also feature prominently in the cover artwork which we have viewed online at your website. The chapters concerning our clients are littered with inaccuracies and are self evidently grossly defamatory of our clients. Publication of these chapters would be unlawful. Furthermore our clients have not consented to being included in the book or to their images being used to

SCHILLINGS 41 Bedford Square, London WC1B 3HX
Tel 020 7034 9000 · Fax 020 7034 9200
Email legal@schillings.co.uk · Online www.schillings.co.uk · DX Number 89265 (Soho Square 1)

Regulated by the Solicitors Regulation Authority

189971_6

promote the book. Such unauthorised use of our clients' images constitutes an infringement of our clients image rights as well as the tort of passing off.

None of the allegations were put to our clients by either Beautiful Books or by its author Steven Machat. Had this been done you would have been advised of the utter falsity of the allegations. Should you seek to publish the book, the failure to act in this manner will give rise to a claim in aggravated damages.

There is no truth whatsoever in the numerous unfounded and grossly defamatory allegations made in the chapters, which include inter alia the following:

1.   An allegation that Sharon Osbourne tried to bribe Mr Machat into releasing Ozzy Osbourne from a recording contract.

2.   The allegation that Sharon Osbourne bleeds Ozzy Osbourne for commissions.

3.   The statement that Sharon Osbourne required sexual behaviour from her road crew.

4.   The offensive statement that Sharon Osbourne was a sexual predator of teenage boys.

5.   The offensive statement that our client is a racist who refused to do business with black people.

6.   The allegation that our clients acted fraudulently in the legal proceedings brought by Bob Daisley and Lee Kerslake. In fact, our clients successfully defended claims brought by Messrs Daisley and Kerslake.

7.   The allegation that Sharon Osbourne filed false allegations of assault against Ozzy Osbourne in order to obtain control over his accounts and money.

8.   Our clients worshipped the occult and had a black magic altar on their tour bus.

9.   The allegation that Ozzy Osbourne is a talentless musician with no musical credibility.

Schillings
Lawyers

10. The allegation that Ozzy Osbourne misspelt his name on his knuckles. This is demonstrably untrue,

11. The allegation that Ozzy Osbourne was forced to make a financial payment in order to avoid being deported from the US.

This list is not exhaustive. Our clients are clearly entitled to pursue a claim for damages in relation to any publication of the Book, and are entitled to:

1. The withdrawal of the offending chapters.

2. An apology in terms to be agreed with this firm.

3. An injunction preventing further publication of the allegations. An injunction preventing further use of our clients images in connection with the Book or promotion of the Book.

4. A Statement in Open Court to withdraw the libels.

5. Payment of our clients legal costs.

6. Payment of damages in relation to defamation.

7. Payment of damages and/or an account of profits in relation to the infringement of our clients image rights.

In the event of publication, the defamatory statements will cause substantial damage to both of our clients. In addition to general libel damages, our clients are likely to suffer significant financial losses by way of lost broadcasting opportunities, sponsorship opportunities, and reduced ticket, record and merchandising sales. Such damages may run into hundreds of thousands of pounds Our clients will be entitled to recover such damages from Beautiful Books, including any special and aggravated damages caused by publication of the Book in any form. Beautiful Books will also be liable for the republication of any of the allegations made in the Book by any third parties including any media reports of the Book.

Our clients' immediate concern is to ensure the unlawful allegations are not published any further.

In the circumstances, we require from you as a matter of urgency and by no later than 2pm on Tuesday 14th October 2008:

Schillings
Lawyers

1. An undertaking that Beautiful Books will immediately withdraw the offending chapters from the Book, together with any other references which are defamatory of our clients.

2. Confirmation that there are no other references in the Book to our client.

3. An undertaking that Beautiful Books will immediately remove our clients from the cover artwork, and all promotion of the book.

4. An undertaking not exploit the Book in its current form including by way of serialisation. If the Book has already been offered for serialisation, we require a full list of who the serialisation rights have been offered to be provided by no later than 2.00 pm on Tuesday 14 October 2008.

5. A full list of the parties to whom the book has been sent including promotional copies to be provided by 2.00 pm on Tuesday 14 October 2008.

6. An undertaking to provide this firm by 2.00 pm on Tuesday 14 October 2008 with:

   (a) A full copy of the manuscript.
   (b) Details of all pre-orders.
   (c) Copies of any promotional material in relation to the Book.
   (d) Details of any proposed print run and when the book is to be printed.

7. In the absence of the undertaking sought in paragraph 1 above, we require Beautiful Books' formal written undertaking that it fully intends in subsequent proceedings for libel (which will inevitably follow) to rely solely upon the defence of justification and that Beautiful Books intends to prove the truth of identified defamatory allegations made concerning our clients to be true. If that is the case, you should in your response to us identify what allegations you intend to justify and confirm that a director of Beautiful Books is prepared to substantiate any claim of justification with a witness statement on oath that he or she believes the same to be true, and providing the basis for such belief[1].

---

[1] See _Sunderland Housing Company v Baines & others_ [2006] EWHC 2359 (QB)

Schillings
Lawyers

Our clients' attitude to this matter including damages (which will be substantial) will be influenced by the speed and sincerity of your apology and provision of the requested undertakings.

In the event that we do not receive your undertaking by 2.00 pm on Tuesday 14th October 2008 we will instruct our client to pursue an application for a pre-publication restraining order to prevent publication of the offending chapters.

We await your reply as a matter of urgency and reserve all of our clients' rights.

Yours faithfully

Schillings

SCHILLINGS

16 June 2009

Russells
SOLICITORS

Simon Petherick

By E-mail: simon@beautiful-books.co.uk

Regency House
1-4 Warwick Street
London W1B 5LJ

TEL: +44(0)20 7439 8692
FAX: +44(0)20 7494 3582
EMAIL: media@russells.co.uk
WEB: www.russellslaw.co.uk
DX: 37249 Piccadilly 1

OUR REF: L:\6379.003\corr\012.BKH.SA
YOUR REF:

Dear Simon

RE: GODS, GANGSTERS & HONOUR – NTEVEN MACHET

As you know, I have recently completed the re-read of the revised manuscript and attached to this letter is a Schedule identifying those matters which in my view are defamatory unless, of course, they can be justified or be the subject of fair comment. Some of these are repeats of the issues which I have raised before and others are new.

The Schedule should be read in conjunction with my original letter of advice to you of 27 May 2008, which still applies, particularly in relation to the issues of confidentiality where Steven's roles are not clearly delineated. Having said that, the primary claims would be against Steven personally as the publishers owe no such duty.

There are two further people contained in the book who, in addition to those listed in my letter, are, to my knowledge, dead, namely Ahmet Ertegun and Tony Stratton-Smith, so I have not included any references to them in the Schedule.

As to the position of Sharon Osborne, it is clear that many of the matters of which she made complaint have either been withdrawn or satisfactorily dealt with but as you will see from the Schedule, there are still several issues which cause me concern which will need to be justified or be capable of fair comment. Given her stance to date, it may well be that she will threaten to issue once more but whether she does remains to be seen. I personally do not know of any case where she has actually gone all the way and given evidence, which she would have to do here.

As I have already mentioned to you, I do not think that it is appropriate to send the re-draft to Schillings, as this will inevitably lead to redrafting and censorship. However, you are obliged

PARTNERS:
A.J.English, B.K.Howard, C.D.Organ, M.E.Sinnott, S.M.Tregear, S.M.Espien, G.A.Maude, P.W.Smith, C.A.Gossage, J.P.Reid.
This firm does not accept service of proceedings by email. / Regulated by the Law Society.

CONSULTANTS:
A.D.Russell E.J.Wyllie.

to give them three clear business days' notice of your intention to proceed with publishing the book and in doing so, are probably obliged to respond to the matters contained in Schillings' letter of 16 October 2008. Whether this should be done by this firm or your insurer's solicitors will much depend upon whether your insurers are prepared to support the book following the libel report enclosed herewith.

No doubt once you have had an opportunity of reviewing the above and the enclosure you will let me have any further comments you may have.

With all best wishes.

Yours sincerely

BRIAN HOWARD

Enc

CHAPTER	PAGE	INDIVIDUAL	ALLEGATION
3. Voodoo Child	16	Rita Lee	Heroin addict – this will need to be justified. — *Research on words*
4. One Day You'll Understand	20	Jimmy Page	That he was obsessed with the old black magic guru (Aleister Crowley). Unless this can be justified, I would prefer the word "*interested*" rather than obsessed.
	27/28	Sly Stone	Drug taking. — *Research*
	30	Allen Klein	Accused of misleading (whether knowingly or otherwise) artists in order to obtain them as clients. Whilst Allen Klein's business matters have been the subject matter of numerous writings and litigation (i.e. The Rolling Stones), this allegation will need to be justified. — *Message wording*
6. Gangbangers, Guns & Crystal Meth	41	Tom Sizemore	Numerous allegations of drug taking and other illegal activities – all of which I believe would be well documented in the past but will need to be justified. — *Research*
7. Games Without Frontiers	61	David Geffin/ Ed Rosenblatt	Allegation of dishonesty in accounting to artists by reason of pressing records in Portugal. I would suggest deleting the words "*short change the artists by paying them*" and insert '*pay the artists*'.
	68	Gail Colsen	An allegation that she did not act in the best interests of her artists – this would need to be justified or be the subject of fair comment. — *Message*

8. The Bitch	69	Joan Collins	An allegation of racism. If SOL -
11. Death of a Ladies Man	87	David Geffin/Cher	A relationship of convenience to promote their own ends. Given their known association, it can probably be dealt with under fair comment. — *fair comment*
12. It's a Kind of Magic	91/92	Rick Smith	An allegation that he took and supplied drugs (repeated elsewhere). Given that he appears to be Steven's business partner, I doubt whether any action will be taken even if it were untrue. — *ovc*
14. The Devil Gets to Play the Best Tunes	110	Adam Tinley	An allegation of drug taking – this has been well documented in the past. — *research*
15. Hi, My Name is George Bush	124	Quincy Jones	Being two-faced and hypocritical. *Message*
	128	Karl Rowe	An allegation of dishonesty and hypocrisy – this will need to be justified in the light of his previous denials. *delete para*
16. On The Road	133	Rick Smith	A supplier of drugs (see 12 above).
	134	John Waite	An allegation of drug taking – I believe that his drug addiction has been well documented in the past but needs to be checked. — *research*
	136	EMI Records	An allegation that they paid for a brothel and therefore participated in corrupt practices. Given how long ago this event occurred, it is unlikely that anyone would be able to

			identify the unnamed executives. Furthermore, I doubt whether the new owners of EMI would have any interest in this. *OK*
17. We Do Not Understand Your Problem	139	Yellowman	Drug addict – again, I believe this to be well documented but would need to be justified. *Maybe*
18. Who's Afraid of Don Arden	143	Sharon Osborne	Her dog peeing under the desk of Myron Roth – implication of bad conduct – however, this appears to be capable of justification following Farrer & Co's conversation with Myron Roth. *OK*
	149	Sharon Osborne	Not acting in the best interests of Jet Records/her father, Don Arden – would need to be justified. *police phrase* *fair comment (so far this is as said)*
	153	Sharon Osborne	Acted cruelly towards her father and would grind both him and Jet Records into dirt by spending. *fair comment – she spread two musicians against Jet*
	154	Sharon Osborne	Oral sex with William Mamone. This will need to be justified (which Mr Mamone seems willing to do). *get email from William*
	155	Sharon Osborne	Drug taking in her offices – needs to be justified. *fair comment – check her back*
	155	Michael Rosenfeld	An allegation of drug taking. *delete? check with Steven*
20. Heading South	165	Denny	Drug supplier. *need justification. Steven?*

3

Chapter	Page	Name	Comment
20. Heading South	165	Denny Brewington	Drug supplier.
26. The Birth of the Queen of Hearts	209	Sharon Osborne	An allegation of bribery – this will need to be justified.
	212	Sharon Osborne	Bleeding dry Don Arden and his Jet empire – against, a need to justify but could also be fair comment. *— delete*
	212	Sharon Osborne	*"Sharon wasn't remotely interested in Ozzy, either as a business proposition or as a lover"*. This is going to be very difficult to justify given that it is not a factual assertion but a matter of opinion. It can therefore only be subject to fair comment. At the moment I do not see how this opinion can be reasonably formed on the facts contained in the book, even if she did initially have a passion for Tony Iommi. The sentence implies that she is hypocritical and is perhaps living a lie. This will need to be re-phrased. *— (handwritten)*
	216	Ozzy Osborne	Spelling his name incorrectly – in the context I doubt that this can be defamatory. *OK*
	222	Sharon Osborne	Acting in a duplicitous manner by instigating claims of Kerslake and Daisley against Jet – this will need to be justified, preferably by one of both of the individuals involved. *(handwritten)*
	223	Sharon Osborne	An allegation of attempted assault/GBH/murder by running over Don Arden. This is a very serious allegation that will need to be justified and if not, removed. Were there any independent witnesses as Don can obviously not be called! *(handwritten)*
	224	Sharon Osborne	Deliberately damaging Ozzy's career – again a difficult allegation to justify. *— delete*

[handwritten marginal note: judgement call]

	227		Does Steven still have this tape? If so, it should be listened to.
27. My Wake Up Call	230/ 236	Rick Smith	Drug taking and supplying (repeat of 12). OK
	240	Bobby Brown	Drug taking – this has been well documented in the past, as have his convictions. — research
	243	Allen Grubman	An allegation that he does not act in his clients' best interests because he is *owned* by the labels. I suspect that despite this, Allen Grubman would not sue as it would open up all his deals.
	245	Allen Grubman	Repeated allegation of him being owned by the labels.
28. Try Being Straight	249	Clive Davis	An allegation that he is connected with the Mob and provided drugs. Unless Steve Tyler is willing to attest to the latter, I would remove the allegation. — need evidence
29. The Troubled Troubador	250	Barry Manilow	An allegation of being gay – I do not know whether this is true or not but if Barry Manilow has denied it in the past then this could give rise to a claim. OK
	253	Leonard Cohen	An allegation of hypocrisy – a devout Buddhist and yet really interested in business. This is a repeated theme. Again, justification will need to be proved.
	254	Leonard Cohen	Conspiracy to evade tax (the same allegation is made of Phil Spector but given his status, I doubt that you need to worry about this).

[Handwritten annotations:]

Do Steven & hasn't he still got it?

it's true! Check with Steven.

research – check out the Lynch/civil case

5

	254	Leonard Cohen	Conspiracy to evade tax (the same allegation is made of Phil Spector but given his status, I doubt that you need to worry about this).
	257	Kelly Lynch	An allegation of theft. — *She was convicted of theft*
	266	Kelly Lynch	A liar.
31. The Most Hateful Man	273	Al Sharpton	The first sentence is gratuitous and can only be defended on the basis of fair comment of his activities, which will need to be justified. — *message?*
	277	Al Sharpton	Drug taking and drug supplying. — *search*
32. Working out with Donny Osmond	286	John Waite	Drug taking (see 16 above).
33. The Crazy World of Gangsta Rap	305	Tru-life	Drug dealer.
	314		Lyrics from "*My Neck, My Back (Lick It)*" will need to be given a credit to the publisher.

Subject: Legal stuff
Date: Thursday, 18 June 2009 16:25
From: Simon Petherick <simon@beautiful-books.co.uk>
To: Steven Machat <smachat@gmail.com>

Dear Steven

There are some things we need before we go to print, all of which I think should be pretty easy, and most of which you are best placed in the US to deal with:

change name to Max

1. The fact your ex partner ~~Rick~~ supplied drugs – do you have easy corroboration of that?
2. Can you ask William Mamone to send an email confirming that he agrees the following statement in the book is true: "Mamone told me only this year that he never fell for Sharon's charms, even if he took the car. He also told me that she was very quick to give head – she unfastened his pants quicker than anyone. Plus, she was good at it."
3. Do you know whether the lawyer ~~Michael Rosenfeld~~ is still alive? On page 155 you say that he took blow when he should have been checking your contract, and we'd need a view on whether he might be someone who could come out and bite us?
4. Same goes for Denny Brewington – we allege that he supplied drugs. What position is Brewington in now? Would he have a go? Can we justify the allegation?
5. When you say on page 222 that Sharon "instigated the claim" by Kerslake and Daisley against Jet – have we got evidence that it was her that instigated it?
6. Don's tale on page 223 that Sharon tried to run him over – you got any proof of that? By the way, I'm hopeful you're going to come back from America with a copy of his tape! In the book you do say that Don gave you the tape – how come it's now with this lawyer guy?

Think that's it at the moment.

Will send revised cover over to you and Mischa soon. All going well, hope you're well over there.

s

Simon Petherick
Publisher
www.beautiful-books.co.uk
Tel: 00 44 (0)20 7734 4448
36-38 Glasshouse Street

Say "the ELO lawyer

Schillings

Lawyers

Beautiful Books Limited
36-38 Glasshouse Street
London W1B 5DL

For the attention of Simon Petherick
By email, by fax and by hand

Our Ref: JK/JO/an/O0042/008
10 October 2008

ON THE RECORD
URGENT - NOT FOR PUBLICATION

Dear Sirs

SHARON AND OZZY OSBOURNE

We act for Sharon and Ozzy Osbourne.

We have been instructed that Beautiful Books Limited ("Beautiful Books") plan to publish a book titled *"Gods and Gangsters"* by Steven Machat on 30th October 2008 ("the Book"). The Book is advertised at Beautiful Books' website and is available for pre-order at several on line retailers including Amazon and Borders.

Last night, at 17.42, copies of chapter 11 and 21 of the Book were emailed to our clients' office by your Publisher, Mr Simon Petherick.

The two chapters of the Book which we have had sight of focus upon our clients, who also feature prominently in the cover artwork which we have viewed online at your website. The chapters concerning our clients are littered with inaccuracies and are self evidently grossly defamatory of our clients. Publication of these chapters would be unlawful. Furthermore our clients have not consented to being included in the book or to their images being used to

SCHILLINGS 41 Bedford Square, London WC1B 3HX
Tel 020 7034 9000 · **Fax** 020 7034 9200
Email legal@schillings.co.uk · **Online** www.schillings.co.uk · **DX Number** 89265 (Soho Square 1)

Regulated by the Solicitors Regulation Authority
Partners: Rachel Atkins · Gideon Benaim · Ros Christie-Miller · John Kelly · Keith Schilling · Simon Smith

189971_6

promote the book. Such unauthorised use of our clients' images constitutes an infringement of our clients image rights as well as the tort of passing off.

None of the allegations were put to our clients by either Beautiful Books or by its author Steven Machat. Had this been done you would have been advised of the utter falsity of the allegations. Should you seek to publish the book, the failure to act in this manner will give rise to a claim in aggravated damages.

There is no truth whatsoever in the numerous unfounded and grossly defamatory allegations made in the chapters, which include inter alia the following:

1.   An allegation that Sharon Osbourne tried to bribe Mr Machat into releasing Ozzy Osbourne from a recording contract.

2.   The allegation that Sharon Osbourne bleeds Ozzy Osbourne for commissions.

3.   The statement that Sharon Osbourne required sexual behaviour from her road crew.

4.   The offensive statement that Sharon Osbourne was a sexual predator of teenage boys.

5.   The offensive statement that our client is a racist who refused to do business with black people.

6.   The allegation that our clients acted fraudulently in the legal proceedings brought by Bob Daisley and Lee Kerslake. In fact, our clients successfully defended claims brought by Messrs Daisley and Kerslake.

7.   The allegation that Sharon Osbourne filed false allegations of assault against Ozzy Osbourne in order to obtain control over his accounts and money.

8.   Our clients worshipped the occult and had a black magic altar on their tour bus.

9.   The allegation that Ozzy Osbourne is a talentless musician with no musical credibility.

10.   The allegation that Ozzy Osbourne misspelt his name on his knuckles. This is demonstrably untrue.

11.   The allegation that Ozzy Osbourne was forced to make a financial payment in order to avoid being deported from the US.

This list is not exhaustive. Our clients are clearly entitled to pursue a claim for damages in relation to any publication of the Book, and are entitled to:

1.   The withdrawal of the offending chapters.

2.   An apology in terms to be agreed with this firm.

3.   An injunction preventing further publication of the allegations. An injunction preventing further use of our clients images in connection with the Book or promotion of the Book.

4.   A Statement in Open Court to withdraw the libels.

5.   Payment of our clients legal costs.

6.   Payment of damages in relation to defamation.

7.   Payment of damages and/or an account of profits in relation to the infringement of our clients image rights.

In the event of publication, the defamatory statements will cause substantial damage to both of our clients. In addition to general libel damages, our clients are likely to suffer significant financial losses by way of lost broadcasting opportunities, sponsorship opportunities, and reduced ticket, record and merchandising sales. Such damages may run into hundreds of thousands of pounds Our clients will be entitled to recover such damages from Beautiful Books, including any special and aggravated damages caused by publication of the Book in any form. Beautiful Books will also be liable for the republication of any of the allegations made in the Book by any third parties including any media reports of the Book.

Our clients' immediate concern is to ensure the unlawful allegations are not published any further.

In the circumstances, we require from you as a matter of urgency and by no later than **2pm on Tuesday 14th October 2008**:

1. An undertaking that Beautiful Books will immediately withdraw the offending chapters from the Book, together with any other references which are defamatory of our clients.

2. Confirmation that there are no other references in the Book to our client.

3. An undertaking that Beautiful Books will immediately remove our clients from the cover artwork, and all promotion of the book.

4. An undertaking not exploit the Book in its current form including by way of serialisation. If the Book has already been offered for serialisation, we require a full list of who the serialisation rights have been offered to be provided by no later than 2.00 pm on Tuesday 14 October 2008.

5. A full list of the parties to whom the book has been sent including promotional copies to be provided by 2.00 pm on Tuesday 14 October 2008.

6. An undertaking to provide this firm by 2.00 pm on Tuesday 14 October 2008 with:

    (a) A full copy of the manuscript.
    (b) Details of all pre-orders.
    (c) Copies of any promotional material in relation to the Book.
    (d) Details of any proposed print run and when the book is to be printed.

7. In the absence of the undertaking sought in paragraph 1 above, we require Beautiful Books' formal written undertaking that it fully intends in subsequent proceedings for libel (which will inevitably follow) to rely solely upon the defence of justification and that Beautiful Books intends to prove the truth of identified defamatory allegations made concerning our clients to be true. If that is the case, you should in your response to us identify what allegations you intend to justify and confirm that a director of Beautiful Books is prepared to substantiate any claim of justification with a witness statement on oath that he or she believes the same to be true, and providing the basis for such belief[1].

---

[1] See _Sunderland Housing Company v Baines & others_ [2006] EWHC 2359 (QB)

Schillings
Lawyers

Our clients' attitude to this matter including damages (which will be substantial) will be influenced by the speed and sincerity of your apology and provision of the requested undertakings.

In the event that we do not receive your undertaking by **2.00 pm on Tuesday 14**[th] **October 2008** we will instruct our client to pursue an application for a pre-publication restraining order to prevent publication of the offending chapters.

We await your reply as a matter of urgency and reserve all of our clients' rights.

Yours faithfully

Schillings

SCHILLINGS

FARRER&Co

Schillings
Solicitors
DX 89265 (Soho Square 1)

Your reference	JK/JO/an/00042/008
Our reference	JCP/kp
Direct telephone	020 7917 7217
Direct facsimile	020 7405 2296
Direct email	jcp@farrer.co.uk

13 October 2008

By Fax: 020 7034 9200
By Post

Dear Sirs

Your clients: Sharon and Ozzy Osbourne
Our client: Beautiful Books Limited

We have been instructed by Beautiful Books Limited following receipt of your letter dated 10 October.

We are taking our client's instructions and will revert to you shortly in relation to the matters raised in your letter. We note the unilateral deadline that your letter of 10 October has set. We anticipate responding to you by that deadline, failing which we will be in contact tomorrow morning to seek an extension of time to respond.

Yours faithfully

Farrer & Co LLP 66 Lincoln's Inn Fields London WC2A 3LH Telephone +44 (0)20 7242 2022 Facsimile +44 (0)20 7242 9899
DX 32 Chancery Lane Website www.farrer.co.uk

Farrer & Co LLP is a limited liability partnership registered in England and Wales, registered number OC323570, and is regulated by the Solicitors Regulation Authority. FARDM1-968458.1
A list of the members of the LLP is displayed at the above address, together with a list of those non-members who are designated as partners.

Schillings

Lawyers

Jay Williams, Esq

By email: jay@swns.com

Our Ref: JK/JO/jo/O0042/008
Your Ref:

13 October 2008

ON THE RECORD - NOT FOR PUBLICATION

Dear Mr Williams

SHARON and OZZY OSBOURNE

We act for Sharon and Ozzy Osbourne.

Thank you for bringing the two chapters of the Gods and Gangsters book concerning our clients (the "Book") to their attention. Our clients have not agreed to be featured in the Book and nor have any of the allegations in the Book been put to our clients.

Your concerns about the Book are well placed. The Book is grossly defamatory of our clients. Furthermore the allegations are highly offensive, wholly untrue and lacking in any foundation. In addition to giving rise to a substantial claim for libel the publication of such allegations would be contrary to section 1 of the PCC Code of Conduct as to accuracy.

You should be aware that separate legal action has been taken by our clients in relation to the Book requiring amongst other things the withdrawal of the chapters concerning our clients.

Naturally we trust that now that you are on notice that the allegations are grossly defamatory of our clients that you will not republish the allegations. We must point out however that the republication of the allegations by you would give rise to a libel claim against yourself and South West News Services.

SCHILLINGS 41 Bedford Square, London WC1B 3HX
Tel 020 7034 9000 · Fax 020 7034 9200
Email legal@schillings.co.uk · Online www.schillings.co.uk · DX Number 89265 (Soho Square 1)

Regulated by the Solicitors Regulation Authority
Partners: Rachel Atkins, Gideon Benaim, Paul Christie, Michael John Kelly, Keith Schilling, Simon Smith

190747_1

Schillings
Lawyers

Our clients are grateful to you for bringing the manuscript to their attention. Given your actions to date, we trust that you will not republish the allegations. On that basis, we would be grateful if you will confirm by no later than **4pm on Tuesday 14 October 2008** that you will not republish any of the allegations made about our clients in the Book in any form.

We look forward to receiving such confirmation. We must of course reserve all of our clients' rights.

Yours faithfully

SCHILLINGS

Schillings
Lawyers

Farrer & Co LLP
DX 32 Chancery Lane

By facsimile: 020 7405 2296

Our Ref: JK/JO/AN/O0042/008
14 October 2008

Dear Sirs

SHARON and OZZY OSBOURNE

We note that despite you having advised in your letter of 13 October 2008 that you anticipated responding by today's deadline you have failed to do so. The deadline set was entirely reasonable especially given the fact that:

(a)   The allegations complained of are of the most serious order; and

(b)   your client is still promoting the Book for sale both on its website and elsewhere with a publication date of 30 October 2008 and it appears taking pre-orders.

The failure to provide a substantive response in the required time is unacceptable, and speaks volumes as to the veracity of the chapters complained of and the numerous outrageous and defamatory allegations. Please confirm what steps your client took to verify the allegations made with the author, Steven Machat. Please also confirm whether the author is the same Steven Elliot Machat who was placed on 3 years probation with a 2 year suspension with the Californian State Bar on 2 May 2002 following irregularities in the maintenance of client funds in trust.

We note that you intend to provide a substantive response by 2.00 pm tomorrow 15 October 2008 and that in the interim your clients will not take any steps to progress the publication of the book. We await your reply and also

SCHILLINGS 41 Bedford Square, London WC1B 3HX
Tel 020 7034 9000 · Fax 020 7034 9200
Email legal@schillings.co.uk · Online www.schillings.co.uk · DX Number 89265 (Soho Square 1)

Regulated by the Solicitors Regulation Authority
Partners: Harris, Atkins, ander, Burbury, Red Christie, M..., the H..., wom Scharoz, Simon Smith   191111_4

Schillings
Lawyers

require you to confirm by return and in any event by 2.00 pm tomorrow the following:

1. Have copies of the Book already been printed? If so, how many copies have been printed?

2. What is the proposed date of manufacture of the Book i.e. when is the print run of the Book scheduled to commence and how many units are proposed to be manufactured?

3. Has the Book been serialised with any media organisation. If it has please confirm to whom and on what date it is due to be serialised and whether it is proposed that any of the allegations made concerning our clients are intended to be included in such serialisation. If they are please specify which allegations are intended to be serialised.

Finally, we note that you have requested that your firm be given notice in the event that an application is made. We assume therefore that you are instructed to accept service of proceedings on behalf of Beautiful Books Limited, but please confirm that this is the case.

We await your reply as a matter of urgency, and in any event by no later than 2.00 pm, Wednesday 15 October 2008. In the absence of undertakings, we reserve our client's right to seek urgent interlocutory relief.

Yours faithfully

SCHILLINGS

FARRER&Co

Schillings
Solicitors
DX 89265 (Soho Square 1)

Your reference	JK/JO/an/00042/008
Our reference	JCP/MXP/vs
Direct telephone	020 7917 7217
Direct facsimile	020 7405 2296
Direct email	jcp@farrer.co.uk

15 October 2008

By Fax: 020 7034 9200
By Post

Dear Sirs

Your clients: Sharon and Ozzy Osbourne
Our client: Beautiful Books Limited

We refer to our letter of yesterday in which we promised you a response to the detailed matters raised in your letter of 10 October by 2pm today. We have now taken our client's instructions and are in a position to respond.

We also acknowledge safe receipt of your letter of yesterday evening. Our letter of 13 October specifically left open the possibility of us requiring more time. Indeed, having received our letter of 13 October, you should have anticipated we would send our letter of yesterday saying a substantive response would not be sent in accordance with your arbitrary deadline. We should make it clear, that it is not 'unacceptable' as you claim for our client to take longer than the arbitrary deadline you chose to set. It was not in a position to instruct us until Monday. Given we have had no previous involvement in this matter, it is not unreasonable for us to take 48 hours to address the substantial matters you complain about.

General Comments

The Book is not an account of events based around your clients and Don Arden. It is Mr Machat's account of his career and the events to which he was party to. Your clients' involvement in his career is of course limited and this is reflected in the Book.

rer & Co LLP 66 Lincoln's Inn Fields London WC2A 3LH **Telephone** +44 (0)20 7242 2022 **Facsimile** +44 (0)20 7242 9899
32 Chancery Lane **Website** www.farrer.co.uk

or & Co LLP is a limited liability partnership registered in England and Wales, registered number OC323570, and is regulated by the Solicitors Regulation Authority. FARDM1-966695.1

FARRER&Co

Schillings
15 October 2008

Whilst your letter of 10 October suggests that the allegations in the Book, in relation to which you complain, concern recent events, chapters 11 and 21 concern events that largely took place in the late 1970s and early 1980s. The Book is, at least in part, a historical account of Steven Machat's career in the music industry and accordingly the allegations you and your clients have identified relate to events that need to be seen in that context, rather than in the light your letter seeks to portray them.

Claim for Passing Off and Breach of Image Right

It is accepted that your clients feature on the cover of the Book. It is not accepted that they feature prominently: they are just two faces at the rear of a group of 28 well-known faces. The use of headshots of your clients' on the cover does not even begin to approach a position whereby your clients can claim passing off. There is also no claim for infringement of your clients' "image rights" since there is no separate tort of image rights recognised in English Law.

Claims in Defamation

We note the numerous claims made in defamation. It is denied that any of the allegations contained in the Book are defamatory of your clients and in each instance the author and publisher are satisfied that the claims made in the Book about which your clients complain are true. In relation to some of the issues complained of, you have manufactured alleged defamatory meanings when, on proper analysis, the words complained of do not bear and cannot bear the meanings you seek to ascribe to the passages.

While our client and the author stand by the veracity of the Book's content, the Book is not about your clients. It does not therefore wish for the Book's publication to be delayed or de-railed by your clients' complaint. Therefore, not withstanding our client and the author's belief that all those matters complained of can be justified — and in the little time that we have had to address the issues raised, we have spoken to individuals who support and who would testify to the truth of the matters

FARRER&Co

Schillings
15 October 2008

complained of in respect of which they have knowledge our client is prepared for reasons of commercial expediency to remove certain non-essential extracts in the Book. For the avoidance of doubt, this is not an admission that those matters that our client is prepared to remove are untrue and not capable of justification, but that it is simply more expedient to exclude certain matters and have the Book published.

Taking each of the allegations you refer to in turn:

1. Our client and Mr Machat stand by Mr Machat's recollection of the incident described on page 127 of the Book. In any event, the incident Mr Machat describes on page 127 does not bear the meaning you seek to attribute to it. Accordingly we do not agree that this passage is defamatory. It is quite clear from the way Mr Machat describes the incident on page 127 that Sharon Osbourne did not try to bribe Mr Machat. Rather it is obvious she wanted to enter into a business transaction – to cut a deal - by offering to pay Mr Machat the sum of $500,000 for "*all the books and records about Ozzy including the Princess Productions Corporation stuff and Jet Records shit*".

2. Our client and Mr Machat stand by Mr Machat's recollection of the incident described on page 129 of the Book. In any event, the passage on page 129 does not bear the meaning you seek to attribute to it. Accordingly we do not agree that this passage is defamatory. Mr Machat says on page 129 that "*Sharon would be able to bleed Ozzy for commissions on merchandising and touring*" (our emphasis). It does not say that Sharon did in fact "*bleed*" Ozzy Osbourne as you claim, whether in this passage or elsewhere.

3. In accordance with what we say above about removing certain passages our client will remove the following words from page 137 of the Book:

   "*Plus Sharon required sexual behaviour with her road crew at her whim*".

FARRER&Co

4. As with 3 above, our client will remove the following words from page 140 of the Book:

    "Sharon would do anything to embarrass her father and Don Arden recalled one of his most humiliating moments at a formal dinner in an LA hotel restaurant. Don was sat at the table with Meredith and the mother of Andy William's road manager who starts off on a rambling story. She started telling them about this Beverley Hills lady from England who had picked up her under-age grandson who had just ran away from home. Don knew in his heart that there could only be one punchline: the pick-up lady was none other than his own daughter. He was correct. Everyone in LA knew this open secret. Sharon had a reputation for picking up teenage boys off the street and taking them home with her to fuck, which Don also admitted to me. In fact, Sharon flaunted it".

5. Our client and Mr Machat stand by the statements in the Book that refer to Sharon Osbourne making racist comments and the fact that she refused to do business with black people. The events referred to on page 141 are also supported by the fact that in 1999 Sharon telephoned Mr Machat beginning the conversation by calling him "nigger manager". Lisa Machat, Mr Machat's ex-wife, has also confirmed to us that she recalls Sharon making racist comments when speaking with her in the late 1970s/early 1980s including criticising the Machats for inviting "niggers" to their wedding.

6. As with 3 above our client will remove the following words from the Book:

    "In truth, she bought her father's testimony and, more importantly, used the promise that Don could see his grandchildren" (page 280);

    "Coming only a month after her father had coughed his guts to our lawyers this seemed like an incredible coincidence" (page 281);

FARRER&Co

Schillings
15 October 2008

and:

"Don told me that the deal was straightforward: Sharon bought him off and gave him access to the grandchildren in return for sinking the action against Sharon and her meal ticket. Sharon was street-bright and when she had the chance she jumped at recreating herself as this great impresario. No longer does Sharon need Ozzy as her meal ticket" (page 282).

7. Our client will remove the following wording from page 278 of the Book in the same basis as above:

"Ozzy told me that Sharon had filed false allegations of him beating the shit out of her. When he was under arrest, Sharon told him she would pursue the charges unless he gave her control over all his money and accounts. Once he signed on the dotted line, Sharon refused to be a witness for the domestic violence charge. Ozzy called me because he had realised he had no control over his life. Sharon was just riding him to destruction".

8. Our client will remove the following wording from page 137 of the Book on the same basis as above:

"My troubleshooter attorney and good friend the late Arthur Pollack who was sent out to clean up the mess told me that he found an altar which some call black magic on the tour bus. Sharon and Ozzy played with the occult".

9. We cannot find any reference in the book to where Mr Machat claims Ozzy Osbourne is *"a talentless musician with no musical credibility"*. Indeed, on page 133 of the Book, Mr Machat states quite clearly that Ozzy Osbourne had *"a lovely voice"*. In any event such a reference

FARRER&Co

would appear to amount to comment and it is a view open to anyone to form without having to face the threat of legal proceedings as a result of making such a comment.

10. We do not accept that saying Ozzy misspelt his name on his knuckles is capable of being defamatory of him. The fact that 30 years later his name is correctly spelt on his knuckles (or, indeed, does not appear at all) is nothing to the point. You have also chosen to extract a sentence from its context and therefore seek to create a wholly misleading picture. As you will know from reading the Book, the relevant passage actually sets out Ozzy's explanation to Mr Machat that he, Ozzy, would be a difficult person to manage, not least because of his severe and admitted addiction to drugs. Your clients have made no secret of his severe difficulties with drink and drugs and the 'knuckles' reference was simply an explanation by Ozzy as to what a mess he was in. This is a fallacious complaint.

11. It is well reported that Ozzy Osbourne was arrested in 1982 after urinating on the Alamo in Texas. This he admits and, indeed, one might be forgiven for thinking he has enjoyed the notoriety that accompanied this incident. For your clients to now complain that he was not forced to make a payment to avoid deportation is remarkable. The first thing to note is that the Book does not allege Ozzy was "forced" to make a payment. What the Book actually states is that because his drunken antics had caused such offence there was a risk ("imminent danger") that he would be deported, which one might think none too surprising. As a consequence Morgan Mason suggested the solution was for a donation to be made. The Book also makes clear that the payment was make by Don Arden not by Ozzy. In light of Ozzy's admitted conduct, we fail to see what harm, even if it were accepted, which it is not, that the words complained of could be said to be defamatory, could be caused by reference to a donation (as opposed to being "forced") being made to avoid deportation. In the circumstances an element of contrition might be thought to be a positive step.

FARRER&Co

Schillings
15 October 2008

In relation to those matters where our client proposes to retain in the Book the passages complained of, we confirm, should your clients proceed to apply for an injunction, that our client will submit evidence confirming its intention to rely upon the defence of justification and detail as necessary the evidence it intends to rely upon supported by statements of truth. We rely upon this letter on the question of costs should you proceed with an application.

Please also confirm that your clients will provide the necessary cross undertaking in damages. We understand that such an undertaking would be not less than £500,000.

In the circumstances, we do not agree that your clients are entitled to bring any claim whatsoever against our client arising out of publication of the Book. In the event you do issue proceedings against our client, you should be aware that our client will defend such proceedings vigorously and will seek to recover its legal costs from your clients.

In relation to the demands numbered 1-7 in your letter of 10 October, we respond as follows:

1. See above.

2   The only other chapter in the Book in which substantive reference is made to Sharon or Ozzy is chapter 4. A copy is enclosed. So that you are aware, we have spoken to William Mamone who has confirmed the accuracy of the references to him and Sharon.

3. For reasons already stated, our client will give no such undertaking.

4. We confirm that no serialisation rights in relation to the Book have yet been agreed.

5. To the extent the Book is serialised, it will obviously be made available in line with this letter.

FARRER&Co

Schillings
15 October 2008

6. We do not accept you are entitled to this information particularly having regard to what we say above.

7. See above.

It is our client's intention to proceed with the publication of the Book subject to those matters set out above. Our client will do so as from Friday morning.

Meanwhile all of our client's rights remain reserved.

Yours faithfully

Schillings
Lawyers

<u>PRIVATE AND CONFIDENTIAL</u>
Farrer & Co
DX 32 Chancery Lane

By facsimile: 020 7405 2296

Our Ref: JK/JO/an/M0259/001
Your Ref: JCP/MXP/vs
15 October 2008

URGENT

Dear Sirs

SHARON and OZZY OSBOURNE – BEAUTIFUL BOOKS LIMITED

We refer to your fax of today's date received at 13:54.

Whilst we are not responding in detail to all of the matters set out in your letter at this time, this letter is written to put your client on notice that its persistence with the defamatory allegations and its stated intention to prove as true those allegations that it will not remove from the Book, and in particular the allegation that our client is a racist who refused to do business with black people gives rise to a claim for aggravated and/or exemplary damages. Such allegation is wholly offensive and grossly defamatory. Special damages will undoubtedly be suffered by our client as a result of the publication of this allegation alone, and are likely to be in excess of hundreds of thousands of pounds and may run into millions of pounds in view of our clients' numerous endorsement and television deals.

We also note your arbitrary reference to the cross undertaking in damages on any application for interlocutory injunctive relief as being not less than £500,000. Please specify by return upon what basis your client believes damages would be of that order.

We note that it is your client's intention to proceed with the publication of the book as from Friday morning. You have however failed to answer the specific questions set out in our letter of 14 October and in particular we require your confirmation by return and in any event by 6.30 pm today as to the following:

SCHILLINGS 41 Bedford Square, London WC1B 3HX
Tel 020 7034 9000 · Fax 020 7034 9200
Email legal@schillings.co.uk · Online www.schillings.co.uk · DX Number 89265 (Soho Square 1)

Regulated by the Solicitors Regulation Authority

191737_3

 **Schillings**
Lawyers

1.   Have copies of the book already been printed? And if so, how many copies have been printed?

2.   What is the proposed date of manufacture of the books? i.e. When is the print run of the book scheduled to commence and how many units are proposed to be manufactured?

Your bare assertion that publication of the book will proceed "as from Friday morning" is hopelessly vague and fails to confirm when the print run of the book will commence.

All of our client's rights are reserved.

Yours faithfully

SCHILLINGS

Schillings
Lawyers

Farrer & Co
DX 32 Chancery Lane

By facsimile: 020 7405 2296

Our Ref: JK/JO/AN/M0259/001
Your Ref: JCP
16 October 2008

URGENT UNDERTAKINGS REQUIRED

Dear Sirs

SHARON and OZZY OSBOURNE

We refer to our correspondence in this matter.

You are on notice that the proposed Book is grossly defamatory of our clients. The Book is also littered with inaccuracies and describes events and meetings that simply did not happen and which are patently untrue. For example, the meeting between Sharon Osbourne and Steven Machat as alleged on page 127 of the Book did not happen, she has never met a number of people who Steven Machat claims she met including Mutt Lange, Lisa Dominique and Richard Steckler. Furthermore, Kelly Osbourne was not friends with Steven Machat's daughter.

Your client's persistence with these allegations when it has been notified that they are untrue exposes your client to a claim for aggravated and exemplary damages. Furthermore your client's insistence on maintaining the truth of Stephen Machat's allegations is not only mischievous but hopelessly misconceived. This is especially so given that (as we are aware) in the course of your Mr Pike seeking to substantiate the allegations, he has been told for example that there is absolutely no foundation at all in the highly defamatory allegation that our client was a sexual predator on young boys. For your client to persist, in the face of this confirmation in standing by the truth of the allegation,

SCHILLINGS 41 Bedford Square, London WC1B 3HX
Tel 020 7034 9000 · Fax 020 7034 9200
Email legal@schillings.co.uk · Online www.schillings.co.uk · DX Number 89265 (Soho Square 1)

Regulated by the Solicitors Regulation Authority

191847_8

notwithstanding its "commercially expedient" decision to remove the offending words, only serves to underline the untenable position to which your client still adheres.

In circumstances where your client's own enquiries demonstrate that Mr Machat is prepared to advance highly defamatory allegations without any foundation at all, and has therefore proven himself to be (as we have already explained) an utterly unreliable source, we firmly believe (and we believe that the Court will accept) that your client's continued reliance on the account given by him and his ex-wife to support such outrageous and damaging allegations, including the highly damaging assertion that our client is (or was) a racist, is not only wholly misplaced but also entirely indefensible.

Only after we had asked for details of any other references in the Book to our clients have we been provided today with Chapter 4 of the Book "Life with the Ardens". Again this chapter is littered with inaccuracies and there is no truth whatsoever in the numerous unfounded and grossly defamatory allegations made in this chapter which include, without limitation, the following:

1. The allegation that our client would act in such an unprofessional manner as to allow her pet dog to defecate on a record company executive's desk during a signing meeting and risk losing an important record contract. This incident did not happen.

2. The allegation that Sharon Osbourne was so unprofessional that she failed to collect a substantial cheque from a promoter following an ELO show in Michigan as she could not be bothered to collect it. This incident did not happen. Our client was not involved with this show.

3. The allegation that our client sought to use company funds to purchase a convertible Mercedes for William Mamone in order to obtain sex is simply not true. Your clients reliance on William Mamone as a credible source is misguided.

4. The allegation that our client had perpetrated an expenses scam on Jet Records involving fake invoices.

5. The allegation that our client used unlawful drugs and had a drug habit which involved sharing a drug dealer with Steven Machat and obtaining drugs from the Ebony boutique in London. These allegations are not true. We have verified with Richard Chemel that these allegations are entirely

false and that furthermore our client did not attend his wedding. This further evidences the unreliability of Steven Machat, and the fantasy that your client is seeking to portray as fact.

Your client's reliance on the author who has demonstrably written such wholly inaccurate and defamatory allegations is entirely misplaced and wreckless.

We have previously provided your client with an illustrative and non exhaustive list of defamatory allegations in relation to Chapters 11 and 21 of the Book. Despite that notice, your client states that it intends to press ahead with publication of these allegations. You should note as follows:

1. The meeting in 1984 at page 127 of the Book did not happen. In fact, Ozzy Osbourne had severed his links with Jet Records a number of years prior to 1984 and neither of our clients have, to their knowledge, seen Mr Machat since on or around 1981. If your client maintains that this meeting took place please confirm exactly what date and where your client alleges the meeting took place.

2. The allegation that Sharon Osbourne bleeds Ozzy Osbourne for commissions is false. Although as his manger our client could charge Ozzy commission, she does not in fact, and has never charged Ozzy Osbourne commission, as Ozzy is her husband. Furthermore the meaning you seek to ascribe to these words in your letter is entirely artificial and does not stand up to scrutiny.

3. The offensive statement allegation that Sharon Osbourne is, or was, a racist who refused to do business with black people is untrue. It is denied that our client made the comments attributed to her. Sharon Osbourne has not met Richard Steckler who Steven Machat alleges she went out of her way to alienate along with his clients.. This allegation must be withdrawn immediately.

4. The allegation that Ozzy Osbourne is a talentless musician with no musical credibility. An example of this is seen in Mr Machat's assertion that "the real creative power behind the throne lay with a trio of session musicians". Ozzy Osbourne is an extremely well respected musician credited with being a pioneer in his genre.

5. The allegation that Ozzy Osbourne misspelt his name on his knuckles. This is demonstrably untrue by looking at any picture of Ozzy Osbourne

over the years as he had his knuckles tattooed whilst he was a young man. Is your client seriously suggesting that our client had a spelling error corrected on his knuckles?

6. The allegation that Ozzy Osbourne was forced to, or made a financial payment in order to avoid being deported from the US is denied. No such payment was made. As an indicator of the quality of Mr Machat's memory of this time, Ozzy and Sharon Osbourne were not in his offices the day after the Alamo incident. They were in the middle of a tour in Texas. Nor did our clients discuss this matter with Steven Machat.

These illustrations provided are not exhaustive and all rights are reserved.

Our clients have not been given a proper opportunity to review the numerous allegations made against them in the Book and all rights are reserved in that regard.

In view of the limited time that our client has had to review the offensive chapters it simply is not possible to set out all defamatory allegations and untruths arising out of the book. To the extent that any particular allegation has not been addressed in this letter no admissions are made and we reserve all of our clients' rights to advance such claims going forward.

The use of our clients' photographs on the front of the Book is clearly intended to suggest to potential readers that our clients are both featured in the Book and endorse the Book. Why else would your client have included them on the front cover. Our clients object to being used to promote you clients Book in this way and being linked to the title of the book Gods and Gangsters. As to your suggestion that there is no claim for passing off or infringement of image rights, we refer you to the case of *Irvine and Talksport* which recognises this cause of action. In the absence of your agreement to remove our clients from the front cover of the Book our client is entitled to seek injunctive relief to prevent the false portrayal of them as approving of and endorsing the Book and for passing off.

Undertakings Required

1. Now that you are on notice of these matters and the fact that these allegations are untrue we require your client's undertaking that these allegations will not be published and that all such allegations and any

Rita Lee : Heroin addict

1) Book : Travesti : Sex, Gender and Culture Among Brazilian Transgendered Prostitutes.

P. 174.   Google Books

2) www.cliquemusic.com.br/en/Artists/Artists.asp?Status = ARTISTA &~~Status~~ Nu_Artista=507 (article)

3) www.brazil.com/pages/p46jan01.htm (article)

4) www.guardian.co.uk/music/2006/may/18/worldmusic.brazil   (article)

5) www.furious.com/perfect/osmutantes.html (article)

Sly Stone : · Drug taking

1) whttp://en.wikipedia.org/wiki/Sly_&_the_Family_Stone   (article)

2) www.bay-area-bands.com/bab00050.htm

3) www.guardian.co.uk/music/2006/mar/19/urban.popandrock

3] Tom Sizemore :- drug taking + illegal activit[y]

(a) Whttp://en.wikipedia.org/wiki/Tom_Sizemore

(b) http://defamer.gawker.com/hollywood/tom-sizem
tom_sizemore_falls-off-the-crystal-wag[on]
154091.php

(c) http://www.starpulse.com/news/index.php/2[0]
02/13/tom_sizemore_talk_about_drugs_paris_h

(d) http://omg.yahoo.com/news/tom-sizemore_arreste[d]
on-drug-warrant/23105

(e) www.chicagotribune.com/topic/entertainment/tom
sizemore-PECLB003715.topic

(f) www.msnbc.msn.com/id/30987647/

4] Adam Tinley :-
www.inmusicwetrust.com/articles/15e01.html

John Waite:—

Found nothing on the
internet

Jellawoman:—

Found nothing on the
internet

7 Bobby Brown :-

(a) http://www.nypost.com/seven/04032008/gossip/pagesix/whitney_drove_me_to_drugs_104751.htm

(b) http://www.msnbc.msn.com/id/4871818/

(c) http://www.people.com/people/article/0,,28152,00.html

(d) http://bipolar.about.com/od/singersmusicians/p/bobby_brown.htm

(e) http://www.nndb.com/people/132/000023063/

---

8 Tru-life :-

Roberto Guzman Rosado, Jr.

his brother :   http://allhiphop.com/stories/news/arc
(wanted for   2009/06/17/21676751.aspx
murder)

Found nothing about him

Beautiful Books

36-38 Glasshouse Street
London W1B 5DL
T +44(0)20 7734 4448

www.beautiful-books.co.uk
office@beautiful-books.co.uk

Adam Wolanski
5 Raymond Buildings
Grays Inn
London WC1R 5BP

18th June 2009

We are...
Beautiful Books
Beautiful Sounds
Bloody Books
Burning House

Dear Mr Wolanski

I am enclosing the penultimate typsetting of the book, Gods Gangsters and Honour, which is the version passed to Mr Brian Howard of Russells for a libel reading. I am also attaching the libel reading report carried out by Mr Howard on that version, and the current final typesetting which includes the text changes we have now made following Mr Howard's advice.

I believe that we are specifically asking you to consider Chapter 18 - Who's Afraid Of Don Arden - and Chapter 26 - The Birth Of The Queen Of Hearts - in relation to correspondence with Schillings which you should by now have been sent by Julian Pike of Farrers.

I would be grateful for a pre-publication assessment from you.

Yours sincerely

Simon Petherick
Publisher

Beautiful Books Ltd is part
of The Beautiful Group plc
Registered in England and
Wales 5208687
Registered office:
117 Sugden Road
London SW11 5ED

OPINION

1.   I am asked to advise as to the libel risks arising out of publication of chapters 18 and 26 of this book.

2.   Schillings, solicitors acting for Sharon Osborne and Ozzy Osborne, wrote to the book's publisher Beautiful Books in October 2008 stating that a number of the allegations made about their clients in a draft of the book were untrue, and that their clients would inevitably sue were they to be published. Many of these allegations have since been removed, but some remain in the text I have been sent. Sharon Osborne is litigious and is likely to carry out her threat to sue if the book provides her with an opportunity to do so, particularly given the history of animosity between her and the author.

3.   My comments on those defamatory passages, and other passages defamatory of Sharon and Ozzy Osborne, are set out below. There are also some passages defamatory of individuals other than Sharon Osborne and Ozzy Osborne which I highlight.

4.   I would of course be happy to advise further if necessary.

Chapter 18 – Who's Afraid of Don Arden?

143   **Allegation that Sharon Osborne let her dog urinate under Myron Roth's desk**

It is arguably defamatory of Sharon Osborne to suggest she permitted the dog to urinate under the desk. I have seen a note of a conversation between Myron Roth and Farrer and Co, during which Mr Roth said he recalled the dog urinating accidentally. I would suggest that the words "so she got it under the desk where bit took its leak" be replaced by "so it ended up under the desk where it took its leak", so as to remove the insinuation that SO *permitted* the dog to do this.

153   Allegation that Sharon Osborne inflicted untold cruelties on her father

This is obviously defamatory of SO. I am informed that it is 'public knowledge' that SO told her children that her father was dead. If there is evidence that SO did this (see comment on 224, below), the allegation is defensible as true. I am also informed that there exists a tape in which her since deceased father spells out her cruelties towards him, though I have not heard this. In the absence of corroborative evidence the allegation is plainly risky to publish.

153   Allegation that Sharon Osborne sought to bring her father to his knees by spending all Jet's money, thereby 'helping it into oblivion'.

This I defamatory of SO. What is the evidence that SO did spend much of Jet's money? If so, what is the evidence for the assertion that she did this in a deliberate attempt to get 'revenge' by destroying the company?

154   Allegation that Sharon Osborne gave William Mamone head

Mr Mammome has confirmed this in a conversation with Farrers (note of 13th October 2008). If he would be prepared to give evidence at trial if necessary, this is defensible as true.

154/5 Allegation that Sharon Osborne and Richard Chemel used to do drugs together

Defamatory of both SO and Chemel. It would seem from the text that the author has personal experience of Chemel taking drugs. Is there any corroboration? This is a potentially risky allegation to make about Chemel. I am also informed that SO had publicly admitted taking drugs in the past, in which case the allegation is safe to publish as far as she is concerned.

2

155   Michael Rosenfeld

Allegation that he took drugs with the author. Is there corroboration? A risky allegation to publish.

155   'the label executives' from CBS

I would suggest amending this to read 'the negotiators' or similar: otherwise there is a risk (albeit a small one) that any of the unnamed (but possibly identifiable) 'executives' could sue.

Chapter 26 – The birth of the Queen of Hearts

209   Allegation that Sharon Osborne tried to bribe Mr Machat into releasing Ozzy Osborne from a recording contract

SO's lawyers have stated in correspondence that this is untrue. There is a very real risk of libel proceedings if this is published. Given the absence of corroboration, the only evidence in support of the allegation is that of the author. I would suggest the allegation be removed.

'Sharon was determined to screw her father and the family firm Jet over the contract of her new husband, Ozzy Osborne'

Defamatory of SO. What is the evidence for this?

214   Harshad Patel

Allegation he had defrauded Jet – defamatory of Patel. What is the evidence? Is Patel still alive?

3

215   William Mammome

Allegation he took drugs – defamatory of Mammome

216   Misspelling of Ozzy's name

The defamatory sting of the original allegation has been removed by the inclusion of the statement that OO may have staged the incident. This is safe to publish.

219-220   Allegation that SO was responsible for the downhill decline in OO's career by firing Kerslake and Daisley

Defamatory of SO to allege that she did this, and that she thereby acted in a 'vindictive, petty and precious' way. Was she responsible for firing them? Is this the reason why OO's career went downhill? If we can prove this, the allegation is defensible as fair comment/ true.

Allegation that SO rewrote history by deleting Kerslake and Daisley from the album credits.

This is defamatory of SO. What is the evidence to support this? Schillings state in their letter of 10/10/2008 that the Osbornes successfully resisted legal proceedings brought by Kerslake and Daisley, though this is presumably a reference to the later proceedings brought by them.

Further, at **221** it is stated that Kerslake and Daisley successfully sued Jet and had their songwriting and performance credits reinstated, and that SO 'instigated' these proceedings because she wanted to discredit her father and lay claim to the master tapes.

The position concerning the Kerslake and Daisley litigation is confusing. Given Schillings' claim that SO and OO successfully resisted claims brought

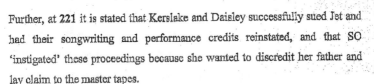

4

by Kerslake and Daisley, it is important to check the correct position. What exactly happened in these proceedings? See also note on **224 ff** below.

222   'Sharon would do anything to embarrass her father. Anything: just read her books'

Defamatory of SO. What is there within her books that is obviously included to embarrass her father?

223   Allegation that SO tried to run over her father

This is very risky indeed, and should be removed in the absence of corroborative evidence.

224   Allegation that SO told her children that her father was dead

Is there corroboration for this (see note to **153** above)? Would Margaux testify that Kelly had been told her grandfather was dead because SO had told her this?

225   Allegation that SO said to her father she wished to piss on her mother's grave

Highly defamatory of SO. Is there corroboration for this? If not, it should be deleted.

225-6 Daisley/Kerslake dispute

The book alleges that there had in fact been a fraud perpetrated on Daisley and Kerslake, and that the 'truth' about this fraud had never surfaced. This is defamatory of SO and OO. Moreover, the book suggests that Don Arden had been persuaded to give false testimony by SO and OO to ensure the truth was never revealed. Similarly at **227** it is alleged that Don Arden told the author that Sharon had bought him off.

5

This is all highly risky, particularly given the specific denial by Schillings that SO and OO had acted fraudulently in these legal proceedings. It would be very difficult to defend a libel claim brought on these allegations given that Don Arden is dead. I would advise that the references to the dispute be rewritten to avoid suggesting that SO and OO acted to suppress the 'truth'.

227 Tape

If Stephen has this tape, it would be helpful to listen to it.

228 Allegation that Sharon Osborne refused her father's wish to be buried alongside his wife

Defamatory of SO. What is the evidence to support this?

24 June 2009

ADAM WOLANSKI

5RB

5 RAYMOND BUILDINGS

6

Ozzy

Invoices

Cald probably beat injunction.

Would probably lose at trial.

Tarantlass

No real problem.

Alamo

No real problem. But we have no evidence of payments made. But unlikely to be sued.

Sharon

Poodle shitting

Roth says it didn't happen.

Brass ring cheque

Unprovable.

Expenses scam

Unprovable.

Trying to buy a Merc for Mamone

Mamone will support? Not sure — he is not reliable

Can't read so couldn't sign affidavit.

Drug dealing

Channel!

Buy out Ozzy recording contract

Cald be construed as negation of bribery ∴ unp

Breeding for commissions

Probably not a prob if rewritten slightly.

Racism

Stickler etc and Richards won't support.

Showbiz News

Sharon Osbourne's messy revenge

Thursday, 11th January 2007, 11:54

LIFE STYLE EXTRA (UK) - Sharon Osbourne used to post her children's faeces to her enemies.

Daughter Kelly has revealed her mother sought revenge on the media by posting her and brother Jack's poo to journalists.

She told Britain's Grazia magazine: "Mum used to make me and Jack s**t in a box, then she'd wrap it up and send it to journalists she was angry with.

"I'd never do anything like that!"

Meanwhile, Kelly has labelled Paris Hilton, Lindsay Lohan and Britney Spears attention-seekers.

The TV presenter is fed up of her friends' embarrassing behaviour and admits she doesn't really know what the trio have in common.

Kelly said: "I want to know what Britney Spears, Lindsay Lohan and Paris Hilton have in common, other than knowing they will be photographed if seen out together.

"Lindsay and Paris are nice girls, but they've got sucked into that lifestyle and are publicity-hungry. Yes, they are my friends but I'm not going to wear matching outfits just so I can get my picture in a magazine. I don't like that world, it's not me."

(c) BANG Media International.

Have something to say about this article?
Then use our comment box to tell everyone else about what you think.
If you have a question, please use the forum.

Comments
Added: 31 Dec '07
"I wish I had you as a mum! Im glad you and Ozzy found each other and raised a family!"
- **Miranda**
Added: 18 May '07
"yo momma is hot yo kelly"
- **yo momma**

Added: 18 Jan '07
"I would love u as na mum im only 11 love u bibi bbz xxxxxxxxxxxxxx"
- **imogen cole**
Added: 18 Jan '07
"hhi love u lol"
- **imogen cole**

All views expressed here are that of the individual and not of this site.

Syndicate: RSS Google MY YAHOO! newsgator

hellomagazine.com

Profiles

SEARCH:

[_____] Go

Ozzy Osbourne

▶ Profile ▶ Gallery

▶ Discography

✉ SEND TO A FRIEND

Rocker, philosopher, bat-biter and family man Ozzy Osbourne has always had a passion for one thing, making music – as loudly as possible. Born in 1948 in Birmingham, young John Osbourne realised early on his destiny would not take him along the academic route. Leaving school at 15, he found a job as a car horn-tester instead.

Supplementing his wages by branching out into burglary, before long he found himself in prison. Upon his release – with a new tattoo reading O-Z-Z-Y across his knuckles and now certain that the music scene was where he needed to be – Ozzy decided to join a band.

Forever in search of the loudest in the land, Ozzy joined and left a series of hard rock outfits before finding Earth, which later adopted the name of an old Boris Karloff movie, giving birth to the legendary Black Sabbath. "As long as there are kids who are pissed off and have no real way of venting that anger, heavy metal will live on," he declared.

The outfit's first record was released in 1970 and a series of hit albums followed. During these years the inimitable Oz also gained a wife, two children, a substance abuse problem and a very bad reputation. His hotel-trashing incidents became infamous and rumours of Satanism began to circulate. "The only black magic we ever got into was a box of chocolates," he insisted. But the media's appetite for "Ozzy's-a-looney" stories was insatiable and his angry outbursts – including one in 1976 when he shot dead a coopful of chickens – didn't help matters.

The following year his father died and Ozzy's enthusiasm for the band waned. His persistent absence from rehearsals eventually resulted in him being fired, and night fell on the Black Sabbath era. Ozzy disappeared into a deep depression and pattern of drug use, which eventually cost him his marriage.

Redemption came in the form of Sharon Arden, whose remarkable combination of talents as a mother, wife and manager would make the Osbournes the first family of rock. The daughter of pop manager Don Arden, Sharon took over the troubled artist's career and, of course, his heart.

He was soon re-established, and the press' obsession with him became as strong as ever. Needless to say, his antics only served to feed their appetite. When a fan threw a bat at him during a stage performance and he famously bit its head off, it wasn't just animal rights activists that branded him as sick and sadistic. Insisting he'd thought it was a rubber toy, the singer underwent treatment for rabies.

Texans joined the ranks of Ozzy-haters in 1982 when he drunkenly relieved himself on part of the Alamo war memorial, earning himself a night in jail and a lifetime ban from the state. It is unlikely his subsequent reflections did much to assuage their anger: "I can honestly say all the bad things that ever happened to me were directly attributed to drugs and alcohol. I mean, I would never urinate at the Alamo at nine o'clock in the morning dressed in a woman's evening dress sober."

When he signed a new contract with CBS Records, his wife suggested he release two doves as a "peace offering" during a party thrown by his old label. He arrived rather intoxicated, however, and opted to bite the head of one of the birds instead. Another day, another media uproar... "Of all the things I have lost, I think I miss my mind the most," he joked.

After undergoing treatment for his addictions, Ozzy continued to find success, winning his first Grammy for the song *I Don't Wanna Change The World* off the 1992 album *No More Tears*. He and Sharon then launched Ozzfest, a touring festival of heavy rock acts, which was so successful it went back on the road in 1998. His status as the "King Of Loud" was confirmed.

It is, however, *The Osbournes* TV show which has made Ozzy, Sharon and teenage children Kelly and Jack, the world's most popular family. The planet's maddest dad is also the "King Of The Ratings," it seems, as his family's not so day-to-day lives continue to fascinate audiences on both sides of the Atlantic. And despite announcing his retirement almost a decade ago, Ozzy shows no sign of slowing down.

- Britney back on top with second No 1 of her career
- Katie Holmes' Broadway turn is 'provocative'
- The Queen gets clicking during Google visit
- French and Saunders bow out with a giggle
- The show goes on for divorcing Madonna and Guy
- 'Sex And The City' stylist's M&S creations hit shops

Your e-mail: | | SIGN UP |

More ways to reach
your audience.

guardian.co.uk

Revealed: how Sharon Osbourne dumps on her critics

Martin Wainwright
The Guardian, Saturday December 9 2006

A larger | smaller

Shit happens, as the increasingly widespread American expression puts it, but if you aggravate Sharon Osbourne it may happen in a particularly targeted and personal way.

The wacky queen of TV talent contests reveals in the Guardian today that she takes an unusually intimate revenge on critics who rile her, especially if they attack her and Ozzy's family.

Offenders can expect a beautiful box from the New York jeweller Tiffany's shortly afterwards, but inside it there are no diamonds but something only Mrs Osbourne can produce. Fighting giggles, she says: "I must have a thing, not about shitting, but about sending it to people. I've done it for an awfully long time. I suppose I find it funny."

Osbourne admits being something of a revenge specialist, a trait which may be inherited from her father, Don Arden, a music impresario and self-styled gangster, who reacted to bad news by threatening to kill whichever of his associates or relatives he considered responsible.

Osbourne's scatological variation on the theme, however, was her own. She describes in a new book how she mixed it with Ozzy's cannabis to try to break his habit, then added it to her father's most precious ornament when he stole from her. She tells the Guardian: "I mean, I don't just do it to anybody. They have to have done something really bad."

No Tiffany boxes have left the Osbourne mansion for a while now, but any harsh critics of the new book might be advised to examine their mail. Osbourne says: "The last turd? Three, no, four years ago. When the first review came out of The Osbournes and it was from a newspaper in America, a very legit one, not the American version of the Mirror or the Sun.

"The journalist said something about my kids being fat and how unappealing that was. And I thought any journalist worth their salt would never write that about children in the society that we live in today." On that occasion, Osbourne recalls, she added a note. "I said, 'I heard you've got an eating disorder. Eat this'."

Sign In | Register

Go to: Guardian Unlimited home   Go

Find someone who likes what you like.

guardian.co.uk

Search: guardian.co.uk   Search

News Sport Comment Culture Business Money Life & style Travel Environment Blogs Video Jobs A-Z

News   Guardian

The Guardian

Home   UK   Business Audio Guardian Weekly The Wrap News blog Talk Search
The Guardian World America Arts   Special reports Podcasts News guide Help Quiz

The Friday Interview

'Eminem sings about killing his wife. My husband actually tried to do it'

Search this site

Go

Sharon Osbourne tells Ian Gittins how she took a booze-soaked rock'n'roll has-been and turned him into a £40m industry

Friday May 25, 2001
The Guardian

Sharon Osbourne doesn't look like a Monster of Rock. The petite, demure 48-year-old holding court in the penthouse suite of London's St Martin's Lane Hotel seems far from the ferocious, ball-breaking figure of legend. She's here from LA to organise a heavy metal festival but she could feasibly be a lady of leisure fixing a whist drive. Until, that is, this self-effacing, almost prim woman begins to tell a few stories. "I see that Eminem gets in trouble for singing about killing his wife," she says, with a tilted grin. "At least my husband actually tried to do it!" Ah, yes. Her husband. For 20 years, Sharon Osbourne has been married to Ozzy, the Black Sabbath singer and heavy rock demigod. It's well documented that their union hit a low in August 1989, when the star returned from playing, ironically, a peace festival in Moscow. Ozzy sank four bottles of complimentary vodka, informed his wife, "I've decided you have to go," and tried to strangle her. "I called the police, and they looked him up," Osbourne reminisces, with an oddly affectionate chuckle. "I didn't press charges but he went into rehab for three months. He was totally insane from all the drink and drugs he was doing, and well, these things happen."

Article continues ▼

► Commercial Banking   HSBC ⟨X⟩
                           The world's local bank

This year Sharon and Ozzy debuted on the Rich List with a joint fortune of £40m. She generated more than half of it, mainly through her artist management activities, as well as the launch and promotion of Ozzfest, the gargantuan heavy metal festival that has toured the US annually for the last six years and hits Milton Keynes this weekend. Osbourne is a pint-sized, dignified, immaculately groomed, middle-aged rock chick. Her accent skips between her native London, Ozzy's doleful Brummie twang and the easy drawl that betrays the couple's last decade in LA raising their three children. Clearly, though, she has a core of pure steel.

Osbourne launched the phenomenally successful Ozzfest in the US in 1996 as an aggrieved riposte to a perceived slight. A few months earlier, she had approached the organisers of Lollapalooza, the achingly hip bohemian travelling rock festival, to ask if Ozzy could play that year's event. "They laughed at the idea," she recalls, eyes burning at the injustice. "They all thought Ozzy was so uncool. So I thought, 'Right, I'll organise my own fucking festival.'" Lollapalooza is long gone now but Ozzfest now grosses $20m every summer in the US, and has launched the careers of Marilyn Manson, Limp Bizkit and Slipknot. This weekend in Milton Keynes, a reformed, creaking Black Sabbath headline over Slipknot, Tool and Papa Roach.

Ozzfest has successfully rehabilitated Ozzy Osbourne from the lost, drugged-up pantomime figure of the late 1980s to a force in music, and nobody who has observed the process seriously doubts that the grounded Mrs O has been his saviour. Her devotion to him is indisputable. "He's a legend," she says, simply. "I admire him and I love him."

Osbourne's early emotional life was troubled. Her father was Don Arden, the legendarily heavy-handed and confrontational avengali manager of Gene Vincent, the Small Faces and, later, Black Sabbath. Arden was frequently accused of violent, bullying tactics by his artists. His daughter followed him into the family business: "If he'd been a butcher, I'd be slicing lamb chops now."

In 1979, Black Sabbath sacked Ozzy. Sharon Arden began to date him, and took over his management from her father. Don Arden was livid. The next time she visited him, his vicious pet dogs savaged her. She was pregnant, and lost the child. "It was horrible," she winces. In the mid-1980s, Don Arden faced trial for false imprisonment and blackmail of business associates, but was acquitted. His son David was found guilty of the same charge and jailed. Osbourne has had no contact with her father for 20 years, but the wounds still fester. "The best lesson I ever had was watching him fuck his business up," she says. "He taught me everything not to do. My father's never even seen any of my three kids and, as far as I'm concerned, he never will."

When Osbourne took over Ozzy's career, the heavy rocker was in a severe drink and drug-fuelled decline and she wasn't too far behind. She was once arrested in LA for drink-driving and bailed out by her best friend, Britt Ekland. Osbourne awoke the next day oblivious to the incident until Ekland jogged her memory. Through these dark days, her shrewd management skills just about kept the family business on the road, but Ozzy and Sharon became notorious for their Sid and Nancy-style alcoholic antics. "Our fights were legendary," she recalls. "We'd beat the shit out of each other. At a gig, Ozzy would run off stage during a guitar solo to fight with me, then run back on to finish the song! We were in the gutter, morally, and I realised that if we both carried on, we'd wind up a washed-up pair of old drunks living in a hovel somewhere. So I stopped drinking."

Nevertheless, she continued to tolerate her husband's excesses. On one occasion she flew to Tokyo to join him on tour. After the show she went ahead to their hotel room, only to be woken hours later by a young Japanese girl climbing into their bed. A drunken Ozzy had forgotten his wife had arrived. "It's funny now," she says, with a tight smile. "It wasn't then."

The Osbournes had three children in the late 1980s, but it took the shock of his 1989 murder attempt to wean Ozzy off the bottle. By then his wife had begun to forge a reputation as one of the most driven and uncompromising managers in the music industry. The industry had confidently expected her to fail, and Osbourne whole-heartedly set about proving them wrong. "People would openly say, 'You and Ozzy won't last," she remembers. "They expected him to have a big-titted blonde trophy wife and he'd got me, a short, fat, hairy half-Jew. I had a lot to fight against."

There were early echoes of her estranged father's modus operandi in the tales that began to filter through the rock world. One promoter was kneed in the groin after defaulting on payments due, and on one irate visit to a company peddling illegal merchandise, she single-handedly trashed their office's computer system. "I felt so ashamed afterwards," she recalls. "Plus I dropped my car keys there, and had to go back to collect them!"

Nevertheless, Osbourne feels she has been popularly vilified because the music industry remains overwhelmingly a man's world. "I'm pretty reasonable," she claims. "If I were a man, I'd just be seen as a great toughie businessman. I'm a woman, so men say, 'Oh, she's a bitch, a whore, a cunt.' I'm afraid it's just what you men do. Plus, I work with my husband, and every woman protects their family." Family unity became even more paramount for the Osbournes in 1992 when Ozzy was diagnosed as suffering from multiple sclerosis, announced his retirement and played a farewell tour. Six months later a second opinion pronounced the diagnosis a false alarm, but the family have only now publicly acknowledged the scare.

As Ozzfest has developed, Osbourne has cut back on her multifarious artist management posts. Last year, however, saw a flash of her famous fiery temper. She lasted only three months in charge of Billy Corgan's Smashing Pumpkins before quitting via a legendary press statement. "I must resign due to medical reasons," it pointedly stated. "Billy Corgan is making me sick." She says: "I shouldn't have said it, but I like to be honest, and after all these years I can't be bothered being politically correct." She's also declined - more politely - recent requests for career guidance from Limp Bizkit's Fred Durst, Guns N' Roses and Courtney Love. "Although I do like Courtney," she says. "She's hysterical."

Osbourne has, however, found time to work with family friend and Wayne's World director Penelope Spheeris on the movie We Sold Our Souls to Rock'n'Roll, a fly-on-the-wall record of last year's Ozzfest. One film highlight is a spirited public debate between Osbourne and a preacher picketing a show, who informs her that her husband is "a practising cannibal". "That's about the one thing Ozzy hasn't done," Osbourne confides, the perfect deadpan comedienne. The movie is currently awaiting cinema release.

Osbourne's career has been powered by one major imperative: to avoid replicating the sins of her father. "I don't want my kids to ever go through what I had to," she says, emphatically and repeatedly. She's particularly concerned that her children respect the metal fans who afford them their privileged lifestyle. "I caught the kids giggling once at some Ozzy fans," she says. "I was so angry. I said to them, 'Don't you ever laugh at those people, because they're the reason we live in the house we do, drive the car we do, and you go to the schools you do. Show some respect." She goes on: "Two years ago, Ozzy was touring America at the same time as the Spice Girls. We stayed at the same hotels. Every day the girls would come out and completely ignore the fans outside. Kids were crying. Ozzy and I were yelling at them, 'You bitches! How can you treat people like this?'" She sniffs: "Mind you, maybe that's why they're in the position they are now."

Nowadays, Osbourne and her 14-year-old son, Jack, trawl LA's rock clubs searching for upcoming bands to play the second stage at Ozzfest. Mr and Mrs Osbourne, however, are largely enamoured of a quiet night in. "We never go out, if we can help it," she confides. "Ozzy likes to watch the History channel. The only music he plays is the Beatles. When we do Ozzfest, our next-door neighbour, Pat Boone, minds the house. We keep ourselves to ourselves." And she laughs, recognising the absurdity of the claim. The Osbournes' marriage has survived farce, tragedy and rich comedy; now, it appears, they've ended up as the heavy metal Terry and June.

The Ozzfest is at the Milton Keynes Bowl on Saturday.

BLABBERMOUTH.NET

LATEST NEWS
NEWS REVIEWS
DVD REVIEWS
CONTACT
SUBMIT NEWS
ADVERTISE
WIRELESS

USER
PASS

☐ Remember Me

LOG IN TO POST

RETRIEVE PASSWORD

SEARCH NEWS

search text Go!

SEARCH CD REVIEWS

search text Go!

NEWS STORY

CLICK HERE TO SUBMIT IT

Last Updated: October 11, 2008 10:35 PM

ICM Agent Fears For Her Life Following SHARON OSBOURNE Assault - Apr. 20, 2003

Talent agent **Renee Tab**, who was involved in a physical altercation with **Sharon Osbourne** in early April, has fired back with new details about the incident at the Koi restaurant in Los Angeles that has resulted in each woman alleging to police that the other assaulted her.

Tab's lawyer, **Najila Brent**, has told **New York Daily News** that, on the night in question, **Sharon** confronted **Tab** about the $15,000 necklace that **Osbourne** has claimed **Tab** absconded with after crashing her New Year's Eve party.

Tab has maintained she won the raffle prize fair and square. According to **Brent, Tab** said, "Are you here to apologize to me?"

Brent said that **Osbourne** "started screaming racial slurs - 'You Persian carpet cleaner! You Iranian [bleep]!'"

The lawyer, who says she will be adding civil-rights charges to the suit **Tab** plans to file, claims **Osbourne** kicked **Tab** and her sister, **Candace**, and "spat three or four times on **Renee**."

Brent also contended that **Sharon** told **Tab**, "I'm going to send someone to slash your face and break your leg."

"**Renee** is afraid for her life right now," said **Brent**, who is seeking a restraining order against **Osbourne**. She added that doctors have told

Sharon Osbourne Bashes Madonna

Thu, 10/26/2006 - 11:46pm by PopSugar

Sharon Osbourne must have something new to promote. The MTV reality star went on Howard Stern to talk trash about Madonna and her recent adoption. In fact, she compares Madge's adoption to purchasing a new LV purse. Wow. We think Sharon can be a riot but sometimes she just wants to cause controversy to promote her book. Here's what Sharon had to say about Madonna & David:

"Please give me a break, it is like getting a Louis Vuitton handbag.

It is a crock of s**t. If she wants to help the kid she should have got the father a little trade going, a fruit stand or something like that and built him a mud hut.

If the kid is sick then get him a doctor, what was the father supposed to do, he can't read or write.

She should have left him in his own culture, that is what I say.

Madonna should have given the money to an orphanage, got them a 24-hour paramedic.

She bought a baby for God's sake."

CHANNEL FOUR TELEVISION
124 HORSEFERRY ROAD
LONDON
SW1 P 2TX
Telephone: 020 7396 4444
Textphone: 020 7306 8691
www.4channel4.com
Direct Tel: 020 7306 8333
Direct Fax: 020 7306 8347
viewerenquiries@channel4.co.uk

25 May 2004

RE: Faces of Four clip - Sharon Osbourne

Please accept my apologies for the delay in reply to your letter of complaint dated 28 March 2004, concerning the above promotional clip, addressed to Right to Reply, As this programme is no longer broadcast, it has been passed to Viewer Enquiries for response

Although the Channel regrets any offence that may have been caused to you as a result of the brief comment made by Mrs Osbourne in this clip, we believe that its broadcast was well within the bounds of audience expectation for material broadcast in this context. We are also confident that the broadcast of this clip is editorially justified under our regulatory codes under OFCOM.

Channel 4 recognises that racist terms should be avoided and, in particular, that insensitive comments or stereotyped portrayal may cause offence. However, although Mrs Osbourne's comment in the clip does play on a stereotype, we do not believe that this stereotype is a negative one in the context. Indeed we have received very few complaints in relation to this clip (the *Faces of Four* campaign itself has been very well received) and believe this would be the view taken by the overwhelming majority of our audience.

The stereotype in question is that of a black man's sexual prowess. The image that black men are more sensitive and satisfying lovers than their white counter-parts was certainly not intended by Mrs Osbourne to be in any way 'racist' or to perpetuate negative stereotypes' of black people. Mrs Osbourne herself is well known for her liberal and all-embracing attitudes. She currently has her own talk-show in the United States (which is shown on Sky One in the United Kingdom) which represents many different racial perspectives and has many celebrity guests of different races. For example in April 2004 Mrs Osbourne had a number of high profile black guests welcomed onto her show including rapper Bow Wow and singer Solange Knowles, comedian George Wallace, Wu-Tang Clan founder RZA, diva Chaka Khan, singer Randy Jackson, Mrs Osbourne also welcomed the Children of Uganda, a group of kids orphaned by AIDS who perform African folk music in the name of AIDS awareness. In February 2004, outspoken TV Judge Mathis helped Sharon celebrate Black History Month.

Accordingly, although we would reiterate our regret that this clip has caused you offence, Channel 4 is confident that the clip was justified in the context in which it was broadcast. We would like to thank you for taking the time and trouble to write to us a Channel 4.

Yours sincerely,

Lucy Brooks
Information Officer
Viewer Enquiries Department

||||| BRANDREPUBLIC

First for advertising, marketing, media and PR

Sharon Osbourne cleared over 'Irish mafia' comments during X Factor

by Jennifer Whitehead, Brand Republic 09-Jan-06, 12:00

LONDON - Sharon Osbourne has been cleared of complaints that she made racist comments after she effectively accused fellow 'X Factor' judge Louis Walsh of being part of the 'Irish mafia'.

Ofcom received complaints from 26 viewers following the episode, which was screened on November 12. In it, Walsh was shown having to decide between booing out Irish girl band the Conway Sisters or London soloist Maria. Walsh chose to eject Maria, for which he was berated by Osbourne.

As she railed against Walsh's decision, she said: "It's a travesty. It's about where they are from and not about talent. It's like the Irish mafia."

Her comments were greeted with a number of boos from the audience, prompting Osbourne to point out that she was part-Irish herself.

Later, Maria graciously defused the situation when she refused to blame Walsh's decision on the Conway Sisters' nationality, and said that she accepted he had decided "from the heart".

Ofcom rejected complaints that Osbourne's comments were racist and unacceptable. In its ruling, it said: "The use of the expression 'mafia' after almost any social group or nationality is a common occurrence in the English language.... We therefore do not believe that the remark was a deliberate attempt to denigrate Irish people in general or that the programme went beyond generally accepted standards."

Osbourne seen throwing glasses of water over Walsh on the following week's show, and the Irishman later briefly quit the show. He was quickly talked around by the third judge, Simon Cowell, and returned to see his mentoree Shayne Ward win the series and score the Christmas number one with his 'That's My Goal' single.

Meanwhile, Cowell became the only judge to boot one of his acts by choice, kicking out the Conway Sisters instead of former stripper Chico.

If you have an opinion on this or any other issue raised on Brand Republic, join the debate in the __Forum__.

Schillings

Lawyers

Beautiful Books Limited
36-38 Glasshouse Street
London W1B 5DL

For the attention of Simon Petherick
By email, by fax and by hand

Our Ref: JK/JO/an/O0042/008
10 October 2008

ON THE RECORD
URGENT - NOT FOR PUBLICATION

Dear Sirs

SHARON AND OZZY OSBOURNE

We act for Sharon and Ozzy Osbourne.

We have been instructed that Beautiful Books Limited ("Beautiful Books") plan to publish a book titled *"Gods and Gangsters"* by Steven Machat on 30th October 2008 ("the Book"). The Book is advertised at Beautiful Books' website and is available for pre-order at several on line retailers including Amazon and Borders.

Last night, at 17.42, copies of chapter 11 and 21 of the Book were emailed to our clients' office by your Publisher, Mr Simon Petherick.

The two chapters of the Book which we have had sight of focus upon our clients, who also feature prominently in the cover artwork which we have viewed online at your website. The chapters concerning our clients are littered with inaccuracies and are self evidently grossly defamatory of our clients. Publication of these chapters would be unlawful. Furthermore our clients have not consented to being included in the book or to their images being used to

SCHILLINGS 41 Bedford Square, London WC1B 3HX
Tel 020 7034 9000 · Fax 020 7034 9200
Email legal@schillings.co.uk · Online www.schillings.co.uk · DX Number 89265 (Soho Square 1)

Regulated by the Solicitors Regulation Authority   189971_8
Partners, Ra... Alleta Gideon Benaim Paul Christe Man ... ... Simon Sm...

promote the book. Such unauthorised use of our clients' images constitutes an infringement of our clients image rights as well as the tort of passing off.

None of the allegations were put to our clients by either Beautiful Books or by its author Steven Machat. Had this been done you would have been advised of the utter falsity of the allegations. Should you seek to publish the book, the failure to act in this manner will give rise to a claim in aggravated damages.

There is no truth whatsoever in the numerous unfounded and grossly defamatory allegations made in the chapters, which include inter alia the following:

1. An allegation that Sharon Osbourne tried to bribe Mr Machat into releasing Ozzy Osbourne from a recording contract.

2. The allegation that Sharon Osbourne bleeds Ozzy Osbourne for commissions.

3. The statement that Sharon Osbourne required sexual behaviour from her road crew.

4. The offensive statement that Sharon Osbourne was a sexual predator of teenage boys.

5. The offensive statement that our client is a racist who refused to do business with black people.

6. The allegation that our clients acted fraudulently in the legal proceedings brought by Bob Daisley and Lee Kerslake. In fact, our clients successfully defended claims brought by Messrs Daisley and Kerslake.

7. The allegation that Sharon Osbourne filed false allegations of assault against Ozzy Osbourne in order to obtain control over his accounts and money.

8. Our clients worshipped the occult and had a black magic altar on their tour bus.

9. The allegation that Ozzy Osbourne is a talentless musician with no musical credibility.

Schillings
Lawyers

10. The allegation that Ozzy Osbourne misspelt his name on his knuckles. This is demonstrably untrue.

11. The allegation that Ozzy Osbourne was forced to make a financial payment in order to avoid being deported from the US.

This list is not exhaustive. Our clients are clearly entitled to pursue a claim for damages in relation to any publication of the Book, and are entitled to:

1. The withdrawal of the offending chapters.

2. An apology in terms to be agreed with this firm.

3. An injunction preventing further publication of the allegations. An injunction preventing further use of our clients images in connection with the Book or promotion of the Book.

4. A Statement in Open Court to withdraw the libels.

5. Payment of our clients legal costs.

6. Payment of damages in relation to defamation.

7. Payment of damages and/or an account of profits in relation to the infringement of our clients image rights.

In the event of publication, the defamatory statements will cause substantial damage to both of our clients. In addition to general libel damages, our clients are likely to suffer significant financial losses by way of lost broadcasting opportunities, sponsorship opportunities, and reduced ticket, record and merchandising sales. Such damages may run into hundreds of thousands of pounds Our clients will be entitled to recover such damages from Beautiful Books, including any special and aggravated damages caused by publication of the Book in any form. Beautiful Books will also be liable for the republication of any of the allegations made in the Book by any third parties including any media reports of the Book.

Our clients' immediate concern is to ensure the unlawful allegations are not published any further.

In the circumstances, we require from you as a matter of urgency and by no later than **2pm on Tuesday 14th October 2008**:

1. An undertaking that Beautiful Books will immediately withdraw the offending chapters from the Book, together with any other references which are defamatory of our clients.

2. Confirmation that there are no other references in the Book to our client.

3. An undertaking that Beautiful Books will immediately remove our clients from the cover artwork, and all promotion of the book.

4. An undertaking not exploit the Book in its current form including by way of serialisation. If the Book has already been offered for serialisation, we require a full list of who the serialisation rights have been offered to be provided by no later than 2.00 pm on Tuesday 14 October 2008.

5. A full list of the parties to whom the book has been sent including promotional copies to be provided by 2.00 pm on Tuesday 14 October 2008.

6. An undertaking to provide this firm by 2.00 pm on Tuesday 14 October 2008 with:

    (a) A full copy of the manuscript.
    (b) Details of all pre-orders.
    (c) Copies of any promotional material in relation to the Book.
    (d) Details of any proposed print run and when the book is to be printed.

7. In the absence of the undertaking sought in paragraph 1 above, we require Beautiful Books' formal written undertaking that it fully intends in subsequent proceedings for libel (which will inevitably follow) to rely solely upon the defence of justification and that Beautiful Books intends to prove the truth of identified defamatory allegations made concerning our clients to be true. If that is the case, you should in your response to us identify what allegations you intend to justify and confirm that a director of Beautiful Books is prepared to substantiate any claim of justification with a witness statement on oath that he or she believes the same to be true, and providing the basis for such belief[1].

---

[1] See *Sunderland Housing Company v Baines & others* [2006] EWHC 2359 (QB)

Our clients' attitude to this matter including damages (which will be substantial) will be influenced by the speed and sincerity of your apology and provision of the requested undertakings.

In the event that we do not receive your undertaking by **2.00 pm on Tuesday 14**[th] **October 2008** we will instruct our client to pursue an application for a pre-publication restraining order to prevent publication of the offending chapters.

We await your reply as a matter of urgency and reserve all of our clients' rights.

Yours faithfully

Schillings

SCHILLINGS

CHAPTER	PAGE	ALLEGATION
1. Childhood	8	Allen Klein	Accused of misleading (whether knowingly or otherwise) artists in order to obtain them as clients. Whilst Allen Kline's business matters have been the subject of numerous writings and litigation (i.e. the Rolling Stones), this allegation will need to be justified.
2. Student Years	13	Eric Kronfeld	Allegation of a general nature of not keeping his word. Again, this will need to be justified.
	15	Tom Paton	Allegation of being gay (which of itself is not defamatory) but allegation of violence would be. Having said, Tom's private life has been exposed by numerous members of the Bay City Rollers and he is therefore unlikely to take any action.
	16	Barry Manilow	Allegation of being gay – I do not know whether this is true or not but if Barry Manilow has denied it in the past then this could give rise to a claim.
3. ELO Grumble	19	Walter Yetnikoff	Appetite for drugs and booze – there are numerous allegations with regard to Walter most of which have either been admitted in his own biography entitled "Howling At The Moon" or have been referred to in such books as "Hit Men" by Frederick Dannen – I therefore think that these allegations can be justified. As a result, I have not commented upon this type of repeat allegation in the manuscript.
4. ELO & the Ardens	25	Steven Machet	Steve details the financial terms of the ELO deal – I do not know whether this has been made public before but it could be a breach of confidence/confidential information.

26	Sharon Osbourne	There are numerous references throughout the book to Sharon which are capable of being defamatory. Again, most of these have been published before but I would recommend a review of her biography to see what she has admitted to. I am also aware that her brother, David Arden, has given interviews to the press (including the News of the World) which details her hypocrisy and her fall out with the family but I am not aware as to whether any action was taken or not in relation to this.
28	Madonna	An allegation that she mimes during the course of live shows. I know that this allegation has been made on several occasions including by Elton John and doubt whether Madonna would sue even if it were untrue.
31	Patrick Meehan	An allegation that he is a gangster – this has been made before particularly in *"Hit Men"*.
32	Michael Rosenfeld	An allegation that he was bribed – given that he is or was a practising lawyer, I think the word *"bribed"* should be deleted and replaced by *"persuaded"*.

5. Genesis

| 34 | Phil Collins | Alleges him to be a *"coke head"* – I am fairly sure that Phil Collins' addiction has been documented on numerous previous occasions but should be checked. |

6. Peter Gabriel & Womad

| 52 | Gail Colsen | An allegation that she did not act in the best interests of her artists. |

8. Phil Collins	56	Steven Machet	Financial details of his deal with Atlantic Records and Virgin Records given – again could be a breach of confidential information.
9. John Waite	58	John Waite – Drug taking	Again, I believe that this has been well documented in the past but needs to be checked.
	60	EMI Records	An allegation that the paid for a brothel and therefore participated in corrupt practices. Given how long ago this even occurred, I doubt whether the new owners of EMI would take any interest in this.
10. Sharon & Ozzy	69	Sharon Osbourne	An allegation that she is racist – I have not seen this allegation before so it would help if some independent research could also be done.
11. New Edition	79	Rita Lee	No comments
12. Rita Lee	79	Rita Lee	Allegation of drug taking – I have no knowledge of this individual.
13. Diabetes	85	Rick Smith	Allegation that he supplied drugs – given that he appears to be Steven's business partner, I doubt whether any action would be taken even if it were untrue.
	88	Colonel Abrams	An allegation that he was leading a secret life, i.e. he was gay but was refusing to admit it. This is a similar type allegation that was made against Jason Donavan who won substantial damages for libel and therefore this will need to be verified and checked.
	90	Bobby Brown	Drug taking – this has been well documented in the past as have his convictions.
	92	Allen Grubman	An allegation that he does not act in his clients' best interests because he is *"owned"* by the labels. I would prefer to use the word *"influenced"* – although it is unlikely that Mr Grubman would sue given his views on litigation.

14. Phil Spector	108	Avril	No comments – especially given his recent criminal trial.
15. Dad's Death	108	Avril	An allegation of theft – this may well be justified given the proceedings in the USA but it would be sensible to review some of the Court orders made.
16. Sharpton	109	Harvey Korn	An allegation of corruption – again, it may well be justified but it would be helpful to review the Settlement Agreement.
16. Sharpton	111	Al Sharpton	An allegation of blackmail.
17. Seal & Adamski	113	Al Sharpton	An allegation of supplying drugs – I suspect, but do not know, that all of these allegations have been made before but where possible should be verified.
17. Seal & Adamski	119	Adamski	An allegation of drug taking – again I believe that this has been well documented in the past.
18. David Copperfield & Claudia Schiffer	125	Rick Smith	A further allegation that he took and supplied drugs.
19. Sharon Osbourne & the end of Don Arden			See general comments above.
20. Bush & his republicans	137	Karl Rove	An allegation of dishonesty and hypocrisy – this will need to be justified in the light of his previous denials.
21. Suge & Death Row	144	Tommy Mottola	An allegation that he is racist – despite the fact that he was married to Mariah Carey.
22. Clinton & Stan Lee Media	147	Peter Paul	An allegation that he was a master forger – I have no knowledge of this person and the assertion will need to be justified.

23. Tom Sizemore		Tom Sizemore	Numerous allegations of drug taking - al of which I believe have been well documented in the past.
24. Leonard Cohen	165	Leonard Cohen	An allegation of breach of promise which will need to be justified.

First set of charges

1. Allegation that SO tried to bribe...

We do not make any such allegation. We suggest that SO made an offer to purchase, which she was in her rights to do.

2. suggestion that she would receive Ozzy merchandising commissions

however SO and Ozzy manage their financial affairs is not what's being discussed.

3. suggestion that so demanded sexual behaviour from kerslake and daisley

Steven confirms that Kerslake and Daisley will confirm this story.

4. suggestion that so acted improperly in kerslake daisley matter

We do not make any such allegation. And it is perfectly reasonable to assume that the damages had they lost might have been so big as to be problematic for them to pay.

5. allegation that ozzy is talentless

We make the precise opposite allegation.

6. allegation that ozzy misspelt his name

We suggest this might have been an ozzy prank.

7. allegation that ozzy was forced to make a financial payment

We don't say this. We say that don arden paid.

8. allegation that sharon tried to buy william a merc

We defend this allegation. William Mamone will consider himself to have been subject to a defamatory remark in relation to this letter.

9. allegation that sharon would allow a records promotion person to take cocaine in her office

We didn't say she allowed it. We said a records promotion man took drugs in her office. Is SO really suggesting that cocaine was not used in record company offices in the '70s?

<u>what they say are examples of steven's inaccuracy</u>

1.　　kelly osbourne doesn't know steven's daughter.

We have plenty of evidence of them being together, of Steven's daughter
Margaux being at Kelly's house and in fact finding prescription drugs to take
with Kelly in Ozzy's medicine cabinet. In fact, Margaux used the prescription
drugs she found in Ozzy's medicine cabinet to get in touch with the doctors
who supplied them, thereby increasing her addiction to those drugs.

2.　　incident relating to Journey - sharon never met Journey

We don't say she met Journey - we say she let her views be known to
Journey. Steven says the Journey people disliked SO so much they refused to
see her.

3.　　many dates are incorrect (they don't say which)

not very helpfully, they don't say which.

4.　　sharon was not in the US in 1984 and wasn't in steven's office on her
own. she says she didn't make him the offer of $500,000

Steven is prepared to accept that it may not have been 84,but if it wasn't, then
it was very close to that, so we will probably change the wording to "mid '80s".
He confirms the meeting took place.

5.　　Don Arden never had any of Ozzy's publishing

Don Arden said this to Steven. If they know something else, then we can
always change the wording to "Don told me he kept the publishing..."

6.　　Ozzy never performed in a band called Blizzard of Oz.

the band was going to be called Blizzard of Ozz, and in fact at the time it was
referred to as that, as a working operation. Publicly, Ozzy did only refer to
himself on the billing. so it's a matter of semantics here more than anything,
it's not evidence of inaccuracy.

7.　　Steven claimed to be on tour with Blizzard of Oz, she says that's not
true.

Steven confirms he was on the tour.

8.　　Alamo claims - Ozzy wasn't with Steven

Steven doesn't say he spoke to Ozzy the day after the incident, he says he spoke to him after the day after the Alamo "drama" was over - meaning once it had all subsided.

9.   ozzy doesn't know steven and has no rapport with him

Not true. Sharon wasn't with Ozzy when he and Steven got to know each other, so Ozzy would have to come to court and state that he didn't know steven.

10.   ozzy has never spoken to steven about dropping acid

Ditto.

11.   steven relies on don arden as a source - he had alzheimer's so he can't be relied upon

Out of interest, I have listened to the tape, which was made in 2000, and this is clearly not a man suffering a wandering mind owing to Alhzeimers. He is cogent, clear and methodical. For them to suggest that Don is not a reliable source is not sustainable.

12.   we suggest sharon abandoned don and left him in a 1-bed flat, whereas sharond claims she paid for a luxury apartment and round the clock nursing

Steven me Don in Don's one-bed flat that Don was sharing with his girlfriend of the time, Meredith. After Don and SO had their reconciliation, he then moved to the apartment to which they refer.

13.   biting head off dove incident

Steven is clear he was present.

14.   myron roth was not the lawyer

Interestingly, we don't refer in the text to Roth being the lawyer. Also, they say he was the Sony lawyer, but Roth was with CBS. They're starting to get confused now!

15.   princess production claim is disputed

I think you have already done research on this, but it is quite clear that in Mar 81 Steven set up the Princess Productions company in Nevada with Sharon as co-officer.

16.   Randy Rhoads was not a session musician he was ozzy's writing partner.

Rhoads did do work as a session musician.

17.   Sharon osbourne did not speak to david mishery

Yes she did. She will need to call Mishery if she is denying this.

[handwritten annotation at top:] She is being defamatory of Stephen (+ William) Sharon + Lisa were friends Mr Machat has no desire to make it about so, but I she wants a fight...

Schillings
Lawyers

<u>PRIVATE AND CONFIDENTIAL</u>
Farrer & Co
66 Linolns inn Fields
London
WC2A 3 LH

By facsimile and email: 020 7405 2296/jcp@farrer.co.uk

Our Ref: JK/JO/an/O0042/008
Your ref: JCP/MXP/66155/1
2 July 2009

Dear Sirs

SHARON AND OZZY OSBOURNE

We refer to your email dated 1 July 2009 timed at 17.47.

That email was unhelpfully sent to our reception rather than directly to the Partner and Associate dealing with this matter who your Mr Pike knows to be our John Kelly and Jon Oakley. Mr Pike has the email details for each of those individuals so we are surprised that this was done.

For the avoidance of doubt, please ensure all future email correspondence is sent to john.kelly@schillings.co.uk, jon.oakley@schillings.co.uk and amanda.norton@schillings.co.uk.

From our initial review of the draft chapters attached to your email the drafts continue to be littered with inaccuracies and contain information which is grossly defamatory of our clients.

There is no truth whatsoever in numerous unfounded and grossly defamatory allegations made in the chapters, which include inter alia the following:

1.   An allegation that Sharon Osbourne tried to bribe Mr Machat into releasing Ozzy Osbourne from a recording contract (p202). This did not happen.

2.   The suggestion that Sharon Osbourne would for her own benefit receive Ozzy Osbourne's commissions on merchandising and touring

---

SCHILLINGS 41 Bedford Square, London WC1B 3HX
Tel 020 7034 9000 · Fax 020 7034 9200
Email legal@schillings.co.uk · Online www.schillings.co.uk · DX Number 89265 (Soho Square 1)

25 MEA
Protecting rights

Regulated by the Solicitors Regulation Authority
Partners: Rachel Atkins · Gideon Benaim · Rod Christie-Miller · John Kelly · Keith Schilling · Simon Smith

289424_1

Schillings
Lawyers

(p204). In fact, Sharon Osbourne has never charged commission to Ozzy Osbourne.

3. The suggestion that Sharon Osbourne constantly demanded sexual behaviour from Bob Daisley and Lee Kerslake (p212). This is not true.

4. The suggestion that Sharon Osbourne acted improperly and/or fraudulently in legal proceedings brought by Bob Daisley and Lee Kerslake. In fact, our clients successfully defended claims brought by Messrs Daisley and Kerslake (p218). Further, the suggestion that our clients, had they lost the litigation would have been unable to afford any damages is ludicrous (p219). On what basis does Mr Machat contend there is any foundation for this allegation at all?

5. The allegation that Ozzy Osbourne is a talentless musician without musical credibility (p208-212). Mr Machat has never attended a rehearsal session or writing session with Ozzy Osbourne. He has no knowledge which allows him to credibly put forward comment on the issue. The allegation that Ozzy Osbourne was not a credible force behind the band in Black Sabbath is put forward as a statement of fact. This is clearly not the case, and if Mr Machat claims it is correct, then he should specify on what basis.

6. The allegation that Ozzy Osbourne misspelt his name on his knuckles (p208). This is demonstrably untrue.

7. The allegation that Ozzy Osbourne was forced to make a financial payment in order to avoid being deported from the US (p213-214). This is untrue.

8. The allegation that Sharon Osbourne had to be stopped by Mr Machat from purchasing a convertible Mercedes for William Mamone in return for sexual favour (p147-148). This is untrue. Your client's reliance on William Mamone as a credible source is, as we have previously stated, misguided.

9. The allegation that Sharon Osbourne would allow a record promotions person to take cocaine in her office at Jet Records (p148). This is untrue.

Further evidence of Mr Machat's extremely unreliable status as a source is demonstrated by the following errors, in what is by no means an exhaustive list.

SCHILLINGS 41 Bedford Square, London WC1B 3HX
Tel 020 7034 9000 · Fax 020 7034 9200
Email legal@schillings.co.uk · Online www.schillings.co.uk · DX Number 89265 (Soho Square 1)

Regulated by the Solicitors Regulation Authority
Partners: Rachel Atkins · Gideon Benaim · Rod Christie-Miller · John Kelly · Keith Schilling · Simon Smith

Schillings
Lawyers

This again demonstrates the work of fantasy that has been written in relation to our clients and how totally irresponsible it would be to proceed to publish the defamatory allegations made by Mr Machat: -

(1) Kelly Osbourne does not know Mr Machat's daughter (p216).

(2) The incident described in relation to Journey is not true (p142-143). Sharon Osbourne has never met the band, Journey.

(3) Many of the dates in the book are inaccurate (various page references).

(4) Sharon was not in the US in 1984 and certainly has not been in Mr Machat's office on her own (p202). The incident described in relation to Jet Records is patently untrue. Sharon Osbourne has been in Mr Machat's office only once with her lawyer, Fred Ansis.

(5) Don Arden never had any of Ozzy Osbourne's publishing as claimed in the book (p204).

(6) Ozzy Osbourne never performed in a band called Blizzard of Oz. He always performed as Ozzy Osbourne (p210-213).

(7) Mr Machat's claim of being on tour with Blizzard of Oz, overseeing a tour in Canada, is absolutely untrue (p205).

(8) The claims in relation to Ozzy Osbourne urinating on the Alamo and the motivation for doing so are untrue (p214). The Texas show was a sell-out. In any event, it would have been physically impossible for Ozzy Osbourne to have been in Mr Machat's office the next day as he was on tour in another part of the country. Furthermore, the suggestion that there is bad feeling between Texans and Ozzy Osbourne is ludicrous. Ozzy Osbourne was given the keys to San Antonio and San Antonio even celebrated Ozzy Osbourne Day.

(9) Mr Machat seeks to portray himself as a friend of Ozzy Osbourne (various). This is not correct. Ozzy Osbourne does not even know Mr Machat and has no rapport with him.

(10) Ozzy Osbourne never spoke to Mr Machat about dropping acid (p208-209).

(11) Mr Machat relies heavily on Don Arden as a source (various page references). It is deeply distressing for our clients for Mr Machat to seek

SCHILLINGS 41 Bedford Square, London WC1B 3HX
Tel 020 7034 9000 · Fax 020 7034 9200
Email legal@schillings.co.uk · Online www.schillings.co.uk · DX Number 89265 (Soho Square 1)

Regulated by the Solicitors Regulation Authority
Partners: Rachel Atkins · Gideon Benaim · Rod Christie-Miller · John Kelly · Keith Schilling · Simon Smith

Schillings
Lawyers

to use as his source Sharon Osbourne's dead father. Such claims can not be substantiated as Don Arden is dead. Furthermore, from at least 2000 onwards, Don Arden was a sick man being cared for by Sharon Osbourne. He had Alzheimer's disease and so any claims Mr Machat attributes to Don Arden cannot be treated as reliable.

(handwritten: because living with mercaptity his girlfriend)

(12) The clear impression is that Don Arden had been abandoned by his daughter and was living in a 1-bedroom LA apartment on the outskirts of Beverly Hills (p219-220). This is not true. Sharon Osbourne paid for Don Arden to stay in a luxury 3-bedroom apartment with 24-hour nursing care and later in a nursing home.

(handwritten: yes he was)

(13) Mr Machat seeks to give the impression that he was in the room when the dove incident occurred (p211). In fact he was not present. Mr Machat even quotes a well known (but untrue) anecdote incorrectly claiming that Ozzy Osbourne had a dead yellow canary in his pocket. His claims are absolutely untrue.

(handwritten: also Pat Siciliano, Myron, ... not Sony)

(14) The suggestion that Mr Machat spoke to Myron Roth, the Sony lawyer, about Ozzy Osbourne is untrue (p211). Myron Roth was not the lawyer looking after Ozzy Osbourne.

(handwritten: we don't say)

(15) The Princess Production claim is disputed (p211). What is the evidence for this?

(handwritten: Mai 81)

(16) Randy Rhoads was not a session musician (p212). He was Ozzy's writing partner. Sharon Osbourne managed Randy Rhoads.

(handwritten: yes he was)

(17) Sharon Osbourne does not know David Mishery and certainly did not speak to him about Death Row Records (p217). This incident described did not take place.

(handwritten: or 99)

In view of the very limited time that our client has had to review the offensive chapters partly as a result of the inexcusable delay in providing copies to us, it simply is not possible to set out all defamatory allegations and untruths arising out of the book. To the extent that any particular allegation has not been addressed in this letter no admissions are made and we reserve all of our clients' rights to advance such claims going forward.

Further, we are unaware what claims are made (if any) as to the status of the Book. Any suggestion that the Book is authorised by our clients would be unlawful and would lead to a claim being made against your client for what would be very substantial damages. Please confirm the position by return.

SCHILLINGS 41 Bedford Square, London WC1B 3HX
Tel 020 7034 9000 · Fax 020 7034 9200
Email legal@schillings.co.uk · Online www.schillings.co.uk · DX Number 89265 (Soho Square 1)

25 YEARS
Protecting rights and reputations

Regulated by the Solicitors Regulation Authority
Partners: Rachel Atkins · Gideon Benaim · Rod Christie Miller · John Kelly · Keith Schilling · Simon Smith

Schillings
Lawyers

Undertakings Required

1. Now that you are on notice of these matters and the fact that these allegations are untrue we require your client's undertaking that these allegations will not be published and that all such allegations and any other defamatory allegations concerning our clients will be removed from the Book.

2. In the absence of your undertaking we require Beautiful Books formal written undertaking that it fully intends in subsequent proceedings for libel (which will inevitably follow) to rely solely on the defence of justification and that Beautiful Books intends to prove the truth of identified defamatory allegations made concerning our clients to be true and that a Director of Beautiful Books is prepared to substantiate any claim of justification with a witness statement on Oath that he or she believes the same to be true and will provide the basis for such belief. This relates to all of the defamatory allegations in the Book.

3. We require your confirmation that these are no other references to our clients in the Book. If there are further references to our clients we require these to be provided by 5.00pm on Friday 3 July 2009. To confirm this, a full copy of the manuscript of the Book should be sent to us by this time.

4. Please confirm how many advance copies of the Book have been distributed, to whom and when.

5. Please confirm whether there have been any discussions regarding syndication, including the names and contact details of any party or parties to those discussions.

We require your response to the above matters as a matter of urgency and in any event by no later than **5.00pm Friday 3 July 2009.**

When responding, please confirm whether you are instructed by each or any of the directors of Beautiful Books and whether you are instructed to accept service on their behalf. In the event that legal proceedings are necessary we anticipate suing each director personally including Beautiful Books' Managing Director as a result of their authorising publication of the defamatory allegations. Their conduct, in failing to meet the requests set out above will of course be assessed by the court and will sound against them in aggravated and/or

SCHILLINGS 41 Bedford Square, London WC1B 3HX
Tel 020 7034 9000 · Fax 020 7034 9200
Email legal@schillings.co.uk · Online www.schillings.co.uk · DX Number 89265 (Soho Square 1)

Regulated by the Solicitors Regulation Authority
Partners: Rachel Atkins · Gideon Benaim · Rod Christie-Miller · John Kelly · Keith Schilling · Simon Smith

exemplary damages. Please also confirm whether you are instructed on behalf of Mr Machat and whether you are instructed to accept service on his behalf.

It is also necessary to place on the record that it is wholly unacceptable to put 2 chapters of detailed information stretching back decades to 2 individuals a matter of days before a print deadline for a book of this nature. We remind you of the Court of Appeal's decision in _Jameel v Wall Street Journal Europe_ that there must be justification to publish allegations without having given the subject a meaningful opportunity to comment unless the story concerns an urgent matter of public interest. There is no such urgency here, other than that generated by your client's own commercial deadlines. Despite that, you and your client have provided copies of the relevant chapters 5 working days before the proposed printing of the Book. There is no allegation made concerning our client which is perishable, or urgent. Your failure to provide appropriate time for comment is a breach of its obligations of responsible journalism in _Reynolds v Times Newspapers_. This breach disallows your client and its directors from any protection it and they might have sought under _Reynolds_.

In the event that your client requires any further time to respond such request can only be considered provided your client agrees to provide an interim undertaking that your client will not take any further steps to progress publication of the Book, unless it has first given our clients through this office at least 3 clear business days notice of its intention to proceed with publishing the Book.

We also require your confirmation that your client will retain all copies of the Book and all documents that are relevant to the dispute including but not limited to emails, distribution lists, manuscripts and drafts of the Book as well as all documents that show what steps have been taken to verify the allegations in the Book.

We await your reply by the deadline and continue to reserve all of our clients' rights.

Yours faithfully

Schillings

SCHILLINGS

SCHILLINGS 41 Bedford Square, London WC1B 3HX
Tel 020 7034 9000 · Fax 020 7034 9200
Email legal@schillings.co.uk · Online www.schillings.co.uk · DX Number 89265 (Soho Square 1)

25 YEARS
Protecting rights and reputations

Regulated by the Solicitors Regulation Authority
Partners: Rachel Atkins · Gideon Benaim · Rod Christie-Miller · John Kelly · Keith Schilling · Simon Smith

re GODS GANGSTERS AND HONOUR

FURTHER OPINION

1.   I have been shown a revised text of this book. The outstanding issues are as set out below.

2.   I would be happy to advise further if necessary.

Chapter 18

147   Sharon repaid her father's indulgence cruelly

This has been toned down from the original allegation of 'untold cruelties'. Given the fact that, as I am informed, it is verifiable that SO told her children her father was dead, this is defensible as fair comment.

147   "It's possible that Sharon believed that by spending Jet's money, she could bring Don to his knees and beg her to help him out"

As long as it is verifiable that SO spent large amounts of Jet's money, this is defensible as fair comment.

Chapter 26

202   Bribe

I would suggest that the following underlined words (or equivalent) into the fourth paragraph so as to render the passage safe:

"Tempting as this offer was, <u>and despite the fact Sharon was perfectly within her rights to make me the offer</u>"...

207   Harshad Patel

This is still risky. I suggest the removal of the allegation of fraud, unless either Patel is dead or we can prove that he committed fraud.

213   Kerslake and Daisley

The book still alleges that SO had K and D's credits removed from the album despite their significant creative contributions to that album. This is fine as long as the description of the outcome of the 1986 litigation at **214**, namely that K and D won and had their songwriting and performance credits reinstated, is correct. Are we certain of this?

218-219   Kerlake and Daisley

The book still alleges that SO persuaded her father to withdraw true testimony by letting him see his grandchildren – the allegation is explicitly made at 220. This is defamatory of her, and would be difficult to prove. I would suggest that the passage be rewritten so as to remove the allegation that SO's made the decision to let her father see the children for this reason. This would involve saying that Don Arden eventually decided not to give his evidence in the case, no doubt because he wanted to achieve a rapprochement with SO and to see his grandchildren, but not alleging that SO deliberately engineered this outcome.

220   Burial

The allegation that SO refused to have her father buried alongside her mother is defamatory of her. I would suggest it be removed.

30 June 2009

ADAM WOLANSKI

CHAPTER	PAGE	INDIVIDUAL	ALLEGATION
3. Voodoo Child	16	Rita Lee	Heroin addict – this will need to be justified.
			We will provide documentary evidence.
	20	Jimmy Page	That he was obsessed with the old black magic guru (Aleister Crowley). Unless this can be justified, I would prefer the word *"interested"* rather than obsessed.
			Word changed as suggested.
4. One Day You'll Understand	27/28	Sly Stone	Drug taking.
			We will provide documentary evidence.
	30	Allen Klein	Accused of misleading (whether knowingly or otherwise) artists in order to obtain them as clients. Whilst Allen Klein's business matters have been the subject matter of numerous writings and litigation (i.e. The Rolling Stones), this allegation will need to be justified.
			Wording changed to accommodate concerns.
6. Gangbangers, Guns & Crystal Meth	41	Tom Sizemore	Numerous allegations of drug taking and other illegal activities – all of which I believe would be well documented in the past but will need to be justified.

6. Gangbangers, Guns & Crystal Meth	41	Tom Sizemore	Numerous allegations of drug taking and other illegal activities – all of which I believe would be well documented in the past but will need to be justified.
7. Games Without Frontiers	61	David Geffin/ Ed Rosenblatt	~~We will provide documentary evidence.~~ Allegation of dishonesty in accounting to artists by reason of pressing records in Portugal. I would suggest deleting the words *"short change the artists by paying them"* and insert *"pay the artists"*.
	68	Gail Colsen	An allegation that she did not act in the best interests of her artists – this would need to be justified or be the subject of fair comment. *Wording changed as suggested.*
8. The Bitch	69	Joan Collins	An allegation of racism. *Wording changed.* Use of the term 'Arabs' agreed not to imply racist views.
11. Death of a Ladies Man	87	David Geffin/ Cher	A relationship of convenience to promote their own ends. Given their known association, it can probably be dealt with under fair comment. *Fair comment.*
12. It's a Kind of Magic	91/92	Rick Smith	An allegation that he took and supplied drugs (repeated elsewhere). Given that he appears to be Steven's business partner, I doubt whether any action will be taken even if it were untrue.

14. The Devil Gets to Play the Best Tunes	110	Adam Tinley *Admerodi*	An allegation of drug taking – this has been well documented in the past. *We will provide documentary evidence.*
15. Hi, My Name is George Bush	124	Quincy Jones	Being two-faced and hypocritical. *Wording changed*
	128	Karl Rowe	An allegation of dishonesty and hypocrisy – this will need to be justified in the light of his previous denials. *Wording changed.*
16. On The Road	133	Rick Smith	A supplier of drugs (see 12 above). *We will provide documentary evidence.*
	134	John Waite	An allegation of drug taking – I believe that his drug addiction has been well documented in the past but needs to be checked. *We will provide documentary evidence.*
	136	EMI Records	An allegation that they paid for a brothel and therefore participated in corrupt practices. Given how long ago this event occurred, it is unlikely that anyone would be able to identify the unnamed executives. Furthermore, I doubt whether the new owners of EMI

Item	Page	Subject	Comment
17. We Do Not Understand Your Problem	136	EMI Records	An allegation that they paid for a brothel and therefore participated in corrupt practices. Given how long ago this event occurred, it is unlikely that anyone would be able to identify the unnamed executives. Furthermore, I doubt whether the new owners of EMI would have any interest in this.
			Agreed.
	139	Yellowman	We will provide documentary evidence.
			Drug addict – again, I believe this to be well documented but would need to be justified.
18. Who's Afraid of Don Arden	143	Sharon Osborne	Her dog peeing under the desk of Myron Roth – implication of bad conduct – however, this appears to be capable of justification following Farrer & Co's conversation with Myron Roth.
			We have Mr Roth's testimony now from Farrer referring to the peeing incident
	149	Sharon Osborne	Not acting in the best interests of Jet Records/her father, Don Arden – would need to be justified.
			We will delete reference.
	153	Sharon Osborne	Acted cruelly towards her father and would grind both him and Jet Records into dirt by spending.
			Fair comment, public knowledge that SO told her children her father was dead, and she

	154	Sharon Osborne	Oral sex with William Mamone. This will need to be justified (which Mr Mamone seems willing to do).
			William will be sending us email confirming the story.
	155	Sharon Osborne	Drug taking in her offices – needs to be justified.
			SO has spoken publicly about taking drugs in the past.
	155	Michael Rosenfeld	An allegation of drug taking.
			We will probably delete this story.
20. Heading South	165	Denny Brewington	Drug supplier.
			We will provide justification.
26. The Birth of the Queen of Hearts	209	Sharon Osborne	An allegation of bribery – this will need to be justified.
			This is SO vs SM. No way of proving either way. Probably leave in?
	212	Sharon Osborne	Bleeding dry Don Arden and his jet empire – against, a need to justify but could also be fair comment.
			We will rephrase.
	212	Sharon Osborne	*"Sharon wasn't remotely interested in Ozzy, either as a business proposition or as a lover"*. This is going to be very difficult to justify given that it is not a factual assertion but a matter of opinion. It can therefore only be subject to fair comment. At the moment I do not see how this opinion can be reasonably formed on the facts contained in the book, even if

		she did initially have a passion for Tony Iommi. The sentence implies that she is hypocritical and is perhaps living a lie. This will need to be re-phrased.
216	Ozzy Osborne	We will rephrase.
		Spelling his name incorrectly - in the context I doubt that this can be defamatory.
222	Sharon Osborne	To be sure, we have added the rider that SM suspects OO may have been playing a trick on him.
		Acting in a duplicitous manner by instigating claims of Kerslake and Daisley against' Jet – this will need to be justified, preferably by one of both of the individuals involved.
223	Sharon Osborne	We will provide documentary evidence.
		An allegation of attempted assault/GBH/murder by running over Don Arden. This is a very serious allegation that will need to be justified and if not, removed. Were there any independent witnesses as Don can obviously not be called!
224	Sharon Osborne	If SM cannot provide evidence, we will remove this.
		Deliberately damaging Ozzy's career – again a difficult allegation to justify.
227		We will delete this reference.
		Does Steven still have this tape? If so, it should be listened to.

	227		Does Steven still have this tape? If so, it should be listened to.
27. My Wake Up Call	230/ 236	Rick Smith	SM in US this week, aiming to get hold of tape.

Drug taking and supplying (repeat of 12).

We will provide documentary evidence. |
| | 240 | Bobby Brown | Drug taking – this has been well documented in the past, as have his convictions.

We will provide documentary evidence. |
| | 243 | Allen Grubman | An allegation that he does not act in his clients' best interests because he is *"owned"* by the labels. I suspect that despite this, Allen Grubman would not sue as it would open up all his deals.

Leave. |
| | 245 | Allen Grubman | Repeated allegation of him being owned by the labels.

Leave. |
| 28. Try Being Straight | 249 | Clive Davis | An allegation that he is connected with the Mob and provided drugs. Unless Steve Tyler is willing to attest to the latter, I would remove the allegation.

Agreed. Unless SM has evidence, we'll remove reference. |

29. The Troubled Troubador	250	Barry Manilow	An allegation of being gay – I do not know whether this is true or not but if Barry Manilow has denied it in the past then this could give rise to a claim. This is OK – no allegation is made.
	253	Leonard Cohen	An allegation of hypocrisy – a devout Buddhist and yet really interested in business. This is a repeated theme. Again, justification will need to be proved. We will provide documentary evidence. SM has plenty of written evidence from the Kelly Lynch case.
	254	Leonard Cohen	Conspiracy to evade tax (the same allegation is made of Phil Spector but given his status, I doubt that you need to worry about this). Ditto.
	257	Kelly Lynch	An allegation of theft. She was convicted of the crime.
	266	Kelly Lynch	A liar. Ditto.
31. The Most Hateful Man	273	Al Sharpton	The first sentence is gratuitous and can only be defended on the basis of fair comment of his activities, which will need to be justified.

8

31. The Most Hateful Man	273	Al Sharpton	The first sentence is gratuitous and can only be defended on the basis of fair comment of his activities, which will need to be justified.
			We will delete reference.
	277	Al Sharpton	Drug taking and drug supplying.
			We will provide documentary evidence.
32. Working out with Donny Osmond	286	John Waite	Drug taking (see 16 above).
			We will provide documentary evidence.
33. The Crazy World of Gangsta Rap	305	Tru-life	Drug dealer.
			We will provide documentary evidence.
	314		Lyrics from "My Neck, My Back (Lick It)" will need to be given a credit to the publisher.
			Agreed.

The Black Sabbath final version.
The epilogue.

Truth. All religions of today's world began as a Black Sabbath.

Sabbath is where you pay homage to your creator. The creator of your mindset. The creator of the matrix which controls your beliefs as to why am I here. What am I supposed to do? What are my limitations of what I can and cannot do?

Ozzy Osbourne is only the latest myth created from the shades of darkness which hide the light. Ozzy made his reputation partaking in a few rituals.

Ritual one was biting the head off a dead dove and spitting the head into the lap of a young lady at the CBS record signing, the distributor of our artist Ozzy Osbourne and his band The Blizzard of Oz.

Ozzy in act two bit the head off of a bat in his concert of darkness in Des Moines Iowa. The sheriff came to town and punished the Oz with rabies shots. Iowa.

Ozzie in act three decides to pee on the street next to the Alamo in San Antonio Texas. A pilgrimage shrine to honor the dead American mercenaries who died protecting the people of a land they called Texas. These people left Mexico and created Texas so they could keep their slaves.

Mexico had outlawed Slavery. The slaves their Christ said was still ok. But still no home run to create the mystical god.

Ozzie became the god out of the ashes of a plane crash that killed the Blizzard of Oz lead guitar player. A man named Randy Rhodes. A player whom the sages of rock n roll believed was the new god of guitar. The plane crashed as it was buzzing the bus that housed Ozzy and his Sharon having, as rumor began, their Satanistic ritual, with Ozzy's Keith Richard known as randy Rhodes dead as a result of the ritual Sharon took the role as the MC and Ozzie was the bard

John Ozzy Osbourne grew up in England. England was the home of the Druids. The Druids my friends was a religious sect whom ruled Brittany (Northern France) and the lands of today's British Isles. Those lands are known as England, Wales, Scotland and Ireland. Remember religion means to bind. Bind you by locking you in to the current system's matrix that controls your thoughts and actions but not your secret desires.

The Druids practiced Black Sabbaths. But they were not the first nor the last. They were only the latest of mankind to do this when they got the power to run their territories.

The rituals of the Druids are simple to enact. But you must believe these rituals to be true or they will not work.

You had to believe in their magic. And their magic was done by their holy priests. And both magicians and priests in the days of old had their serpents as their symbol. Why? Because a snake every year could shed its skin. Therefore defy the rules of nature and appear to have eternal life.

Sacrifices is what mankind did when they needed the god of hell fire to change the way nature was treating a community. Man would build altars and then pour blood over the altar so the god of darkness would give these men and women what they needed to survive their heathen life styles.

The blood was offered because they believed god was merciful and blood would appease god. True.

Notice god here is not capitalized. Because the Creator, my God would never be part of this crystal. This is Satan at his little red riding hood best. A big bad wolf.

The blood of these rituals at the ritual births would start with animals. Then if the favor the blood was supposed to bring did not work it became humans.

Human sacrifices began with the most beautiful and innocent of gods creations. Those being beautiful and young virgins. From the girls the sacrifices would move to the eldest son.

If you choose to disbelieve me read any old writers whom survived the book burning of the Vatican in Europe, Northern Africa and the Middle East as well as Central and South America. Be they Herodotus, Strabo, Cicero and even Mr. Caesar himself to name but only a few. This is how our current societies were built. On Black Sabbaths.

The sacrifice (which really means an offering of the cake), in Britain were chosen first from the criminals then in jail. Or if they had any the prisoners of war those would work too. If those two categories did not exist for the latest ritual someone from the community would step up. Sacrifice their cake, their body to save the community.

Then in those Druids' lands of milk and honey, the sacrificial human lamb was led into the Enchanted Forest of the Robin Hoods of their time. These forests had running streams. Water was needed to purify the spilling of blood.

In the center of the arena, was the rock temple without roof so god had a clear view of the festivities. The Priest was the Master of Ceremonies. The Priest whom was dressed in his judicial robes of white would stop the winds. The Priest would have the trees in his ceremonies extend their spectral arms. These arms that would soon be sprinkled with the blood of an Englishman. You know the fable Jack and the Beanstalk? The English fable. "Fee Fi Fo Fum" begins here. The green giant was none other than the trees reaching down from the skies to get the blood so they could continue use their rise to the god in the sky.

We are not taught what extracts of nature the congregation was eating or drinking as they witnessed this stage performance. But something was definitely given to them as if it is today with beer and peanuts or cracker jacks. Maybe just mushrooms. Mushrooms are all over this land. Magic buses to get you there in the space to believe in this sacrifice.

Birds would not sing. The priest waved his arms like a bigger bird and magical science drowned their screams. No it was now time for the bard to take center stage. The Ozzy of that era.

The bride of death of this ceremony was now brought to center stage. This bride, or victim was made to sing the song of death.

Now with priest dressed in his white gown the ornaments were placed on his body. The priest had a serpent's egg encased in gold wrapped on his body near his heart. Around the priest's neck was the collar of judgment. This collar would strangle the priest, it was said, in case the judgement of death the priest was to enact was wrong.

The priest had on his finger the ring of divination. In his hand was the glittering blade. The guillotine of its day.

Then the bard sang and took the lead. The bard would chant in his blue robe a very solemn dirge. Reminds me of a Hebrew Cantor type of voice. Which is Ozzy's voice tone.

The bard then sang to sinister tones that came out of the harps being played by his blizzard of musicians trained to rain the tunes of death.

Now the priest was hypnotically transformed into god's executioner. The audience mobbed what today we call the pit. Everyone was ready for death to come and save their day.

The altar boys and girls would then come on stage and throw oak leaves, the tree of wisdom they were taught, in mockery of the sacrifice lack of innocence. These branches were scattered all over the altar. About to get their blood.

With the bard and his band playing the tune of death march, in this court of their Crimson King, the priest would raise his blade. But off with his head was not the game.

No, like the bulls who get killed in the bull fights we still have today, this blade, the Priest now a matador, put the blade into the nape of the victim's neck. The dying man, like a bull in those matches would fall to the ground leaking blood. The audience would gather around and in their moment of joy threw new leaves of oaks on the altar.

Then the community would sit and have their death feast. This is the Druids Sabbath.

And so you hear my cries please understand these Druids were not alone. We, mankind are a Black Sabbath. We make war and say god wanted it this way.

We are the real cancer of society. We live in fear knowing what we live is not the big god's way. But we are scared to change the ways we live. Or we too will bear the cross.

Before religion of a Christ like figure, when love was in the air, sacrifices to a god were from the herbs and flowers that the community loved. But then when sin became man's way of life, really what we call the Iron Age era, man offered god blood.

Man in this Iron Age learned to tremble at their own thoughts. Man became a community of thieves. To steal one must lie and at times murder too. New game was being played on mankind. We were made to get the gold and we needed weapons to dig it and steal to keep it.

Man knew they were wrong so they needed god's forgiveness. So they sacrifice their own believing god had a taste for blood.

So for you history lovers or novices I ask you to read the stories of the imperial cultures of our past. And do know Christianity is an imperial religion. Just look what the old bible teaches us to do. Look at the altars used in those days of angry god. Look at the cultures we love. Be they Egyptians, Greeks Assyrians, Nubians, and Romans. History of death with the winner being sanctified as the loser was vilified.

But let us share truth. All cultures of mankind sang these rituals of death plays and their tunes. Getting the picture?

Look at your culture. Scandinavians, Scythian, the

Albanians, German and Franco tribes all cultures based on leadership by follow or die. Let's not leave out the Iberians or the Gauls. Let's move to the Middle East and the Arabs, the Phoenicians they did this too.

Going around our globe let us see that The Chinese and those of the Indian sub-continent cultures had their own song and dance all to take part in their Black Sabbath of their day. Australia and their Aborigines or Maori's sure could dance their tune. And the African tribes had their voodoo black magic too.

Fellow soldiers looking for our way home I ask you a few questions? Why do we do the things we do? We all worship the dark and believe it is the light.

Where is our creator?

When will the myths justifying death and the new god finally end? When will we be a society of equals?

The school of sacred knowledge is here for you.

About the Author

Who is Steven Machat and how does he know so much about what went on?

BD. Steven Machat was born into the music business in the 1950s as the son of Marty Machat, a high-level music industry lawyer. The Machat family were close friends with the Ardens, Don in particular, and Steven became a show business lawyer and entrepreneur himself. Both Marty and Steven Machat represented Don Arden and Jet Records in contractual and legal matters over many years. Steven's recently-released book 'Gods, Gangsters and Honour' contains the most accurate, honest and truthful account of what happened in regards to The Blizzard of Ozz, the band's members, Don Arden, Ozzy and Sharon Osbourne, the details of our lawsuit and its outcome that I've seen in print to date. He saw at first-hand all that went on within Jet Records, the Arden family and the Osbourne connection. This is a book the Osbournes would not want people to read; I highly recommend reading it.